KT-199-116

A Mother's Grief

Thirty Years On

Betty Madill

Other books by the author
Sowing the Seeds of Hope, 1997
One Step at a Time, 2001, also
available as an eBook from Amazon

150th Anniversary of the Catholic Church
in Inverurie, 2002
160th Anniversary of Catholic
Worship in Inverurie, 2012

Published by
Blue Butterfly Publishers
Inverurie AB51 4ZR
Aberdeenshire
Scotland, UK

Betty Madill©February2013

ISBN: 978-0-9573670-1-2

Betty Madill asserts her right to be known as the author of this book under the Copyright, Designs and Patents Act 1988.
All rights reserved. No part of this publication may be reproduced in any format or on any recording devices, without prior written permission of the publishers.

Cover Designed by
Marc Madill©September2012
marc.madill@which.net

Printed by
Witley Press Ltd.
www.witleypress.co.uk

Data Protection

Although this book is a true account of what happened to our daughter and life while living in Rio de Janeiro. Names used within the context of my story have been altered to protect the identity of those people who were there and who played a part in the unfolding of the event within it.

Dedications

This book is dedicated to my family and my many compassionate friends, especially Sandra and Janet, who have continued to support me over these years through this most difficult of journeys.

Thanks also to the many bereaved parents who have encourage me to keep writing to let them and others know we do not have to travel the road of grief alone and that there are always others willing to share the load.

Also to the memory of Lisa and the little ones I was never meant to meet, but also helped to form me into the person I am now.

Acknowledgements

Thank you to Patsy and Jackie who have given their time to proofread the typescript and helped produce a book that will help many, many bereaved parents to find a way forward that suits them and their needs.

Foreword

A Mother's Grief

Over, thirty years ago when my life changed for ever I had no idea of the journey that I had just embarked upon. Then one night, about two months following Lisa's loss, when I was unable to sleep and feeling utterly bereft, I felt inspired by God to write an account of the emotional roller-coaster that my life became as a result of my three-year-old daughter's death. At that point the last thing on my mind was any concept of turning my pain and grief into words on a page that would one day become a published book, but that is what happened, when *'One step at a time/Mourning a Child'* became a reality.

Every night from then on I would get ready for bed – and before turning in for the night I would sit with a notebook and pen and wait to see what would emerge. Within minutes the ink would flow freely and words would tumble onto the pages so rapidly that my hand could just write fast enough as letter by letter the lines were filled with sentences and paragraphs.

It took eighteen years of perseverance and learning the ins and outs of the 'writer's world' before I found a publisher, Floris Books of Edinburgh. Their editor could see what I was trying to achieve by telling my story – to help other bereaved parents to find their own way of dealing with the distress that arises from the death of their child - and he helped me to shape it into the book that it became.

Now, thirty years on, I find myself reflecting on the impact the death of Lisa has had upon my life and that of my family; and on the depths of despair and the stages along the road I have travelled, through the words of this new book. I hope to explore some of the suggestions I made in *'One step...'* to reveal if indeed life did unfold as I had hoped it might, to discuss some of the unexpected issues which arose and show how my life and personality were affected as a direct result of my experience.

Yes, I would have preferred that Lisa had not died. But she did and writing has helped me move forward and enabled me to find a way of getting to grips with the agony that filled my every minute of each waking hour. It helped me to arrive at a point that I never would have believed was possible when I lost her – when I could accept the fact that my daughter was dead and nothing could change that truth, but that her short life need not have been for nothing and her death would not be the final act of her time in the world. Therefore, if my writing down all the 'ins and outs' of my journey helps any other bereaved parent to find a way forward in their grief, then her life and death would count for something and she would be remembered long after the three years and three months of her life.

Chapter 1

A Mother's Grief

Thirty years is a long time in anyone's life and it is frightening how quickly time passes. It is only when we glance back do we realise that we have indeed travelled a long road to where we are now. When I began my path I had no knowledge of how I would get through the first hours never mind a whole life time. In the early days it was impossible to look beyond each day and each new day meant another day beyond the time when Lisa was alive and living with us. I found it agonizing to continue to survive without her to care for and despite the awfulness of the day she drowned it was hard to not relive it over and over, yet the reality was that gradually time crept forward and I was drawn further away from that darkest of days into a reluctant future. I came to realise that since I could not go back to a time where Lisa once lived I had to find ways of enabling myself to accept this and seek methods that would allow me to rebuild a new life, but fears of leaving Lisa behind in my past made this task feel like a necessary obligation rather than a sought-after aim. Like needing to go to the dentist to have a tooth filled – it has to be done, however we know it will not be a pain free exercise. In saying this, I had no idea how much the pain would become part of my very existence, a pain no medicine could dull, a pain that was so real and solid it was impossible to shift, at least it was real and it allowed me to stay connected to Lisa – somehow, it was an emotion I would have to learn to live with if I was to stay sane.

In the depth of my despair I was desperate for anything that would distract my mind, something to make a noise and reasons to get out of the apartment.

Writing became my salvation and protection for my sanity. It gave me a way to remove from my brain the tangle of thoughts which played repeatedly and continually throughout the day; once written onto the pages I was able to leave some of these thoughts there giving, me some measure of relief so that I was more able to deal with each new dawn as it arrived. Yet I was to discover that they were never erased entirely, just set aside for a while. I was also to find out that I would revisit each and every aspect of my loss many more times over the years and also learn that the gaps between each revisit would widen and become less frequent as time passed. Eventually I reached a point when I could actually choose not to go back over it, without feeling guilty about moving on because I also realised that I would never fully forget what I once had and could take myself back there whenever I wanted to or felt the need to, anytime. I had only to see a little girl with blond wispy hair and blue sparkling eyes, hear a particular song, visit a favourite venue or just take time out of my busy life to think of how my life could have been if things had turned out differently all those years ago.

One of the hardest things to get used to each day was the endless silence in our apartment. Anyone who has children knows how constant the sound is until the baby, the toddler, the child, the teenager goes to bed and is actually asleep, which in most households takes all day and with older kids much of the evening too. When Lisa died our apartment became devoid of that constancy of sound, play and chatter. Kevin had been fourteen months old when his sister passed away. He had depended on her as his playmate and had not begun to talk much and I did not, as yet, have the strength of mind to get down and play with him without Lisa being there. There was no longer the endless chatter and questions that all little children of Lisa's age utter most of their waking hours. To solve this problem I would switch on the television just to have some background noise. It did not matter that all the programmes were transmitted in Portuguese (we were living in Brazil at the time) or that I did not understand enough of the language to take in much of what was being televised, but at least the place was no longer silent.

Prior to Lisa's accident, I had taken up these pastimes. When she died we took her home to Scotland so that we could have her funeral in Glasgow, our home city and where she is buried. Now that I was back I was wondering what to do about filling my time. I didn't really know what to do. Then one morning the phone rang and the voice at the other end was that of Peggy Murray, my Bridge tutor. She was phoning to ask if I would be able to make up a four. We had finished the lessons she taught me and several other women some weeks earlier and she had brought a number of them together to put into practice what they had learned. The thought of attending anything remotely social was a challenge and I hesitated about accepting her invitation, but Peggy's gentle voice made me decide to go. As I came to realise some time later, with the wisdom of her years, it was her way of helping me to get out and about. She knew it would stop me isolating myself and would be a source of self-help by giving me a short respite by making my mind think of something other than my grief. She said, 'Don't worry if you cannot come, but it would just be so much better if you did'. Not wishing to let her down, I agreed to go along to her place where the Bridge party was being held. So, after making sure my child-minder was okay about looking after Kevin to allow me to go, I picked up my car keys and drove to Peggy's flat. When I got there I almost changed my mind about ringing the doorbell, but her parting words to me on the phone that morning were, 'it might help', came to mind. The way in which she'd said them and I heard them told me that this woman knew what she was talking about and I needed anything no matter how trivial to stop me from sinking further into the self-pity which was threatening to swamp me. So I rang the bell and waited to be allowed in to what became my next step forward in slowly reconstructing a life without Lisa.

The initial problem that plagued me was that if I was able to do normal things in a routine manner it made me feel that I was leaving Lisa in the past while I had assumed that she would be with me all of my life. And if I was able to do normal things when my life no longer felt normal was I denying that she had been part of our family? Why was I able to function at all let alone drive the car and plan to meet friends? However, I was beginning to learn to move on into the future devoid of her presence and I came to gradually understand that although I could never again hold her in my arms, she would never be far from my thoughts and she would continue to be a very real part of my life. Not in a haunting sense, but as a constant impetus to drive me forward and to live my life to the best of my ability, despite the pain involved, a pain that was never far from the surface, but one I would come to manage. Like someone who has to learn to live with a physical chronic pain brought on by an illness, no matter how much it hurts and however long it takes while getting used to it, yet for the rest of their life, they learn to put up with it, I had to do likewise with the pain I was feeling.

Child bereavement is so unique that for each parent of a lost child their way of dealing with the loss will also be unique. Each will need to find their own unique approach to it, depending on how it affects them and how it impacts upon them and how they subsequently move on. Some parents will be able to discover ways in which to do this. Some will never be able to tackle the overwhelming reality of it and lock it away in the recesses of their minds where it will lie dormant for the rest of their lives. Yet others, like me, will need to revisit it time and time again picking at the scab again and again until we reach a point where we can finally let the wound heal and allow the scar to form as it may. A scar that won't be visible to anyone, but we know it is there and we have no desire to erase it from our hearts.

Our pain is a symptom of the love we have for our children and even though they are no longer living amongst us we still have that love for them which we need to acknowledge, I believe this is why bereavement support groups such as The Compassionate Friends (TCF) are so invaluable. They allow us a place to go where we can talk about our loss, share our pain and recall the love we still have for them with people who understand our need to express ourselves.

This helps us one day I hope, as it has happened to me, to turn a very bad negative life experience into a more manageable one. We can, if we want, again know some sense of happiness despite our ceaseless yearning for our child. For me, I would rather be known as Lisa's well re-adjusted mother than to be seen as a heart-broken woman who has allowed the bereavement to destroy any chance of hope in her life, instead of learning to live despite her loss. We cannot have them back yet we can say and believe that we would rather endure the agony of their loss than not have ever known them. This may not be true for all bereaved parents, but it has been for me.

On entering Peggy's flat there were two tables already set-up, one with four women ready to start playing and the other with three and a vacant seat for me or so I thought at the time. Reflecting back I realise now how clever and perceptive Peggy had been – because if I had ducked-out and decided not to come, she could easily have made up the numbers for the other table. However, since all or most of the women there had also attended the same course of lessons that I had with Peggy, she simple resumed her role as tutor giving us prompts and reminders of the strategies she had taught us as her pupils. I will always have a special place in my heart for this lady, because of her insight and the kindness. She showed me that I need not cope on my own and that it was okay to do normal things. There would be other people like Peggy who would hold out a hand to me to enable me to circulate by extending invitations to me. I learned that it was better for me to be out among people instead of enclosing myself in a cocoon where I could indulge in feelings of self-pity and unhappiness.

That one-off session of Bridge developed into a regular weekly event as many of us signed up to take part in a course of Advanced Bridge lessons. Yet, since settling back in the UK I have never played it again. It served its purpose when I needed it and one day I know I shall play it again and I still have somewhere in my home the basic rules and tips which Peggy gave to all her pupils that will be crucial for me to study when the time presents itself.

The other game I learned to play while living in Rio de Janeiro was Mah-jongg. It is a game that comes from Eastern Asia and was once played throughout China, Japan and other oriental nations. It uses tiles which were originally made from bamboo and ivory although they are now more often made from synthetic materials. After my pleasant experience with my Bridge friends, I contacted one of the women with whom I used to play mah-jongg to ask where they would be meeting; she told me where and offered to take me there. Again I was apprehensive about meeting with these women since I had not heard from any of them since Lisa's loss and did not know whether they would welcome me or not.

I had already, despite it being less than three months since the accident which caused Lisa to lose her life, met with resistance from people I had counted as friends but who for some reason were deliberately avoiding me. I was yet to work out why. I did receive a mixed welcome, some were delighted to see me while others held back a bit but one woman seemed resentful about my attendance. I learned while we were playing that this woman had not long since been told she had some form of cancer and for some reason, which I never did discover, she made it clear from her body language that she would have much preferred it if I had not come. My thoughts on the matter are that I think she needed the other women to be there for her, but they were there for both of us and I hoped that she would draw strength from me and I know I drew strength from her and was glad that the others there could have something else to focus on other than my bereavement. As I felt it was better for them to treat me as they had before the loss and not feel they had to treat me any differently from occasions I was in their company prior to my loss. For the most part this was how the rest of that morning progressed.

My motto for dealing with my loss became, 'take each day as it comes' and to find something to help me and Kevin get through the new day. Sometimes we went out and there were other days I did not have the energy to do anything so we stayed home. Kevin would play on his own and at other times I would sit on the floor and do jigsaw puzzles with him, while the television played in the background to provide the flat with noise. Each hour would seem endless but somehow we got through the days and evenings until sleep allowed my mind to switch off and rest.

Sleep was the only way to rid my mind completely of all the constant 'what ifs' and 'whys' buzzing inside my brain. Yet, in the immediate days after Lisa's death, sleep was hard to find. I would go to bed because that is what people do when it is night time. I would lie in bed beside Dave sometimes hugging each other while the tears flowed. At other times he would be asleep and I would lie awake wanting to shut out the thoughts spinning around in my mind yet not able to switch off. Then in the morning the sunbeams streaming in through the thin curtains would stir me awake and I would be racked with guilt as the thoughts and feelings of the night before would flood my brain yet again and the reality of my life would once again be all too clear. Guilt that I had actually stopped thinking about Lisa while I was sleeping; it was a Catch 22 scenario, sleep helped give respite to my weary mind and body and eased the stress I was under, but feelings of guilt were the punishment for a peaceful night's sleep.

It would take a while before I could accept sleep for the solace it gave me, realising that it could not be avoided and if I was to be the kind of mother Kevin deserved then I had to have the energy to enable me to look after him properly and to be a decent wife to my husband, Dave.

Since it was I who had been with Lisa the day she died I felt that it was my fault that they no longer had a sister and a daughter. Therefore, it fell to me to do my best to strive on and somehow make things easier for them. The short answer was that nothing I could do would ever compensate for Lisa's loss of life. Perhaps if I had been less occupied with chatting to my friend I might have been more aware of Lisa going into the water and if I had, then my beautiful little girl might not have drowned. Yet, a constant source of help was there right from the start even before I was fully aware of it, but without it I could never have survived at all.

On the very first day of our bereavement I demanded that God provide me with the means I would need if I were to continue to exist. Why did I not ask to be taken with Lisa? I do not know, but what I do know is that God has answered me and has been constantly helping me, one way or another, every day and night since. Yes, I have and did pray that she would be revived and often wonder what my life would have been like if she had, but at the time it was clear that she was not going to be and I knew even in those fraught minutes of trying to save her that we were too late and that the only way I would be able to live without her was with help from God.

Chapter 2

What a difference a day makes

At that period in our lives, Dave, Lisa and I were living in Rio de Janeiro. Dave worked for an oil company and had been posted there to work along with other colleagues to explore for oil in the Atlantic Ocean off the coast of Brazil. We came to enjoy living there, but initially it took some adjustments before we settled in a country where they had a very different lifestyle to the one we were used to in Aberdeen, Scotland.

Both growing up not far from the City of Glasgow had given us 'street- cred' that served us well in Rio. Once we had become aware of the potential dangers of just walking about, especially in the Copacabana area, we learned to keep our eyes open and our wits tuned into what was happening around us. We were able to make the most of this opportunity of living in one of the most spirited cities of the world, and Dave was earning a decent salary at the same time. It was not everyone who had the chance we had been given, hence we made the best of the time we had there.

Yes, of course, there were drawbacks to get used to, like the cockroaches that seemed to appear from nowhere the instant there was darkness, the constant tardiness of local people to come to pre-arranged appointments and social gatherings – I learned that Brazilians considered it the height of rudeness to arrive anywhere less than fifteen minutes later than the time at which they were expected; and that they did not see it as bad manners at all. There was also the advice from other women on how to keep myself safe in public when out and about on my own.

Primarily, not to place my handbag on the floor beside my feet whenever I stopped for lunch or a coffee, as in Rio there is no such thing as a free lunch. By putting my bag down at my feet was a signal to men that I was available for the price of a meal, for whatever. In other words, I was an easy pick-up.

Yet, another piece of advice made me shudder, although I don't know if Rio is as dangerous now as it was when we lived there, but I was told at no time whatsoever to leave Lisa alone when out shopping. I had to keep her close by me at all times and make sure I kept hold of her hand in crowded places and at no time to enter a shop while leaving her outside. It had been known for white children to be snatched by kidnappers who would demand a ransom for their safe return or they might be sold on to raise money for whatever the crooks were into whether it was the slave trade or to feed their drug habits. Brazil's economy has improved greatly since the time when we were there and perhaps Rio is different too, and hopefully there has been an effort to address the grinding poverty which was so evident during the early years of the 1980s. Despite all these undercurrents of potential crime, until the day Lisa died, we had truly enjoyed our time there.

The beginning of the year 1983 did not get off to a good start, unlike the previous week when we had a great time celebrating Christmas with lots of friends at a party. Kevin was too young to take part so while he slept in his travel cot, we three enjoyed the fun, ate delicious food and supped drinks along with the rest of the company, many of them being work colleagues of Dave's who had also become good friends. The party was being held in Frank and Ella's flat. Frank had decided to have an alternative take on the traditional Christmas Dinner and had curried the turkey instead of roasting it; in the Southern Hemisphere December is in the middle of summer and in that hot climate curry worked well.

Being a hot evening and as the sun had set Frank had switched on the hosepipe to water the plants of his terraced garden as the temperature had dropped and the flowers would benefit from the

27

quick dowsing. The garden took up much of the balcony area which lay to the left of Frank's main room, the doors to which he left opened to allow people to go out for a breath of air and allow a gentle breeze to waft inside. After giving the plants a quick shower he had placed the hose in such a way so that the water would slowly soak into the ground and saturate it. Perhaps after he'd watered the garden he had intended to turn off the tap, but not before Lisa found it.

We knew nothing of what she was doing until people who had gone out to have some fresh air were coming back in with splashes of water on their clothing. It turned out that Lisa had decided to help Frank by continually showering the plants with the water, but it seemed whenever somebody went over to speak to her they ended up being watered too. Thankfully, none of the guests were bothered about it and all took it with good humour.

I, however, knowing most of them were wearing lovely party outfits and that they might not appreciate standing around with damp clothes on, decided to bring Lisa's 'good deed' to an end. Unknowingly, inadvertently, she had given all of us at that party a happy memory of her that six weeks later would be all we would have of her. Perhaps in time, like me, the other guests would recall this episode with a smile and laugh when they remembered the little girl who watered their outfits as well as the flowers.

The following week we were all assembled together again at another colleague's apartment to see out the old year and bring in the new. This time I wasn't in the best frame of mind. I hadn't realised that there was a dress code for that evening and that everyone was expected to wear an all white outfit. I was aware of the significance in Rio of the month of January. In ancient times Janus was regarded as a god with two faces, one looking back and the other looking forward; as people tend to do when one year ends and a new one is beginning. However, I had not realised that it was customary to wear white on that evening and so I felt rather foolish that I had come wearing something that was very definitely not in keeping with the theme for the party. My mood lightened a bit when more guests arrived and as they were planning to travel back to Britain later that night they had come ready for their trip in casual everyday clothes and were not wearing white either. As midnight was only thirty minutes away, Dave and I decided to take the children home so that we could be in our own place before the New Year began. It was only a five minute drive back from where we were and our two were soon snug in their beds and sound asleep well before the bells were due to ring out.

As we sat with drinks in our hands waiting to cheer in 1983 we heard fireworks being set-off down on the beach front. However, as there were two high-rise multi-storey buildings blocking our view all we could see was the odd rocket exploding in the sky above them. Dave who loves fireworks stood up suddenly and made for the front-door as he had decided to go and have a better look down at the beach leaving me alone while he went out to enjoy himself. Any other time of the year this would not have bothered me in the least, but right then at the end of one year and the start of another I felt abandoned. Especially since all the rest of my family were miles away in different countries. He seemed to have forgotten all about our two little ones sound asleep in their bedrooms, and that I had no choice but to remain in the flat with them to make sure they came to no harm.

A short time later, much sooner than I had expected, I heard his key in the door. He was really apologetic having finally realised what he had done, but for me his apology came too late, the damage in our relationship had happened. It took a long time afterwards for me to sort it out in my mind; that although my husband did love me, a simple thing like a few fireworks – which we could have watched together from our balcony – for a moment meant more to him than I did. He might disagree with this view of that night, but it did nothing to help me believe that I could trust him not to let me down in such a manner in the future. Whether this was a sign of foreboding of a bad year ahead is debatable, but all too soon our lives were about to be blown apart and for us our family-life would never be the same.

Since it was the middle of summer the children were on holiday from nursery school and toddlers' groups, but the new term for Lisa would begin mid-February. Throughout much of the time she had been off nursery I had done very little with her and Kevin. I hadn't made any effort to meet up with their friends' mothers so that the children could play together and was feeling guilty at my lethargy. It was just that much easier to throw open our balcony doors, put out the paddling-pool so that the kids could splash around to stay cool while they played there with their toys. They didn't seem to mind not going out and the weather was so hot that we would only have ended up going to the beach and more than likely become overheated and burned by the sun; and at least we had a ready supply of food and cold drinks and the balcony was a reasonable size therefore most days I would plump for the easier option.

The first Saturday in February gave Dave and me an excellent opportunity to take our two out somewhere nice, but the sun was very strong and I felt that it was too hot to stay outside in it for long, and it was far too nice a day to go walking around a shopping mall so we decided to stay home yet again. Kevin and Lisa seemed happy enough with each other's company that they didn't complain about staying at home. Then on the Sunday, after attending church, we had yet another quiet day at home; and again the children were happy going between the television room and the veranda, playing with their toys and having a great time playing follow-the-leader. Although it was Kevin who was leading Lisa and getting his sister into trouble from time to time, instead of the older sibling leading the younger into mischief.

Once more the paddling-pool was on the veranda and we filled it with water. It wasn't long until the sun warmed the water to a pleasant temperature for the children to sit in when they became too hot. They were really enjoying splashing about in it and using little toy buckets filling them and then allowing the water to pour out into the pool again. Then Kevin, copying Lisa's actions of hitting the surface of the water and causing it to slash upwards, got a little over-excited with his slapping and some water got into Lisa's eyes and she hated anything at all but even more so water getting into them. She started shouting, 'My eyes, my eyes,' and becoming quite upset, but Kevin was really enjoying the game and I had to intervene and settle them down again. He had no idea that what he was doing was causing a problem for Lisa, but I had suggested a different game to do with the water and soon they resumed playing together peacefully. Although, the water had to be topped-up as the splashing game had reduced the depth of it quite a bit.

The veranda was encased by the walls of the apartment block and had a sturdy metal fence of about four and a half feet high, with railings which were too closely set for a child to slip through, although we did lose the odd ball through the bottom as well as through the gaps in the railings. As a result it provided a safe, secure area for our two to play. Even so we didn't allow them free access to it and made sure at least one of us was with them at all times just in case they did try to see if they could squeeze through them, and since our apartment was situated on the fifth floor, there would only have been one result if they had managed to succeed in their experiment.

Altogether that weekend was full of fun and peace and has now become a treasured memory of a lovely family time spent together simply enjoying each other's company while appreciating the sun and at the same time ensuring none of us became overheated. While minding our two little ones between us, Dave and I took the chance to catch up on our reading. There was nothing to hint at what the next day had in store for us. Yet, it has become a time that feels like a little golden nugget worth recalling when times are tough and I struggle to remember what our lives were like once.

Recalling this incident makes me remember the premonition that I had late in 1982. It occurred during the night while I was asleep. I had seen in my dream one of my children falling; the child had nothing on the top half of its body but was wearing something white around their bottom half. Where the child fell had railings, but I didn't know the outcome of the fall as I woke up. I was so disturbed by this vision that I related it to a girlfriend. Whether you believe in forewarning I don't know. However, the dream and what then happened at Sue's place were so uncannily alike. I was glad that I had the presence of mind to tell my other friend about the dream I had months earlier, otherwise I think that I would have really become insane.

The truth was that our lives were soon to become that living nightmare. I don't know if Dave has any hidden memory of that weekend, as he cannot and has never been able to speak of our loss as he decided after about two months that he did not wish to revisit things which only caused him pain and anguish, in regards to Lisa's death. However, I cherish it as I would a precious jewel or keepsake. I hope one day that he will allow his memories to return and then we can remember our little girl together with laughter and with tears.

Monday, 7 February 1983 started innocently enough. Dave had already gone out to work and as I had made no plan to go out with the children, I lay half-awake trying to persuade myself to rise. There was no sound coming from either of the children's' rooms. Although I knew I would need to go out sometime that day to buy groceries and things that Lisa would need to take with her when she resumed

37

nursery the following week I was in no rush to start the day. Then the phone began ringing. At first I did not wish to answer it as I was enjoying my relaxation, but when the ringing persisted I reluctantly picked-up the receiver.

It was my friend Sue whom I had met on my first day in Rio. We had quickly become good friends and my daughter, Lisa and her son, Danny had also become best playmates. Our friendship was sealed still further when we learned that we were both pregnant and that our babies were due to be born a month or so apart. The fact that she happened to be Dave's boss, Charles's, wife was purely coincidental. We were simply friends whose husbands happened to work together but this did not influence our relationship in any way. Both men also developed a friendship quite separate from boss and employee and we were regular guests at each others dinner parties. Sue was also a keen mah-jongg player and we played this once a week with other women who took it in turn to host the game in their homes.

That morning of 7th February, Sue was phoning to invite me to bring the children out to her place so that they could play with hers and we could catch up on each other's news as we hadn't seen each other for a while. She had no plans to go anywhere that day and would appreciate our company. My first instinct was to turn down her invitation, but then something, possibly guilt that I was prepared to allow yet another day go by without taking my children out anywhere enjoyable, made me change my mind so I heard myself saying that I would come, but was not sure if I would bring Kevin, as I thought Lisa would enjoy the day better having Danny to herself; and anyway Kevin much preferred to have a lazy start to his day and was always in a much better frame of mind if he was allowed to wake by himself rather than being bad-tempered if I woke him.

As Lisa's bedroom was further along the hallway than Kevin's, I looked in on him first. If he was awake then I would get him ready and take him along too, but he was still fast asleep so I closed his door again, quietly, and went along to Lisa's. She, too, seemed to be asleep then I realised she was stirring; I went over and said very softly into her ear, 'Do you want to go to visit Danny today, so you can play?' Instantly, she jumped up, still on her bed, full of excitement at the thought of seeing her little playmate. 'Yes!' she said, 'Let's get ready and go'. First we went to have some breakfast and then I took her through to wash and dress her. The style of sink we had in the bathroom meant that she was able to sit on the surround while I sponged her over, as she'd had a bath the night before, this was all she needed to freshen her up. As I looked at my little girl with her hair looking blonder than ever, having been bleached by the sun, I guess, I realised that she was no longer a toddler now but a proper little girl with her very own strong personality, happy and excited because she was going to see her wee pal that day.

I realised that I was going to have to wake Kevin to take him too, but while I finished getting Lisa dressed my home help, Yara, rang the doorbell to be allowed in, she came most mornings to help me keep the apartment in order. She adored my two children. When she saw that Lisa and I were ready to go out, she was happy to look after Kevin, as he was still asleep and she said she would give him breakfast when he woke up. So, after having another look in at him, Lisa and I set off for our day's adventure.

It was another gloriously sunny morning. The sky was very blue with some white fluffy clouds dotted about and a very light breeze wafted in from the sea which lay just about a quarter of a mile to the right of our apartment complex. Although it was still quite early in the day it was obvious that it was going to be another very hot one and I was glad that by the afternoon we would either be back home; or gone off to a shopping mall to get out of the heat and do some shopping before Lisa returned to nursery school. Once Lisa was safe and secure in her car seat, I got into my seat and did up my seat-belt before heading off for a nice morning catching up with both of our friends.

Before to this day I had been struggling with my faith in God. I was no longer sure if I believed that He existed or if I still believed that Jesus Christ was His Son and that He had once lived among men. Living in Rio, where there was a great deal of utter poverty alongside the very rich and affluent people of the same city, made me doubt how a God of love would actually allow this dichotomy to continue, when there was clearly ways to stop it by putting into the hearts of people the aspiration to help their fellow citizens when and wherever they could. However about a year earlier, I had met Hilda who was a committed Christian who soon became a trusted friend. She gave me literature which helped to solve some of the problems I had about my view of God and the ways He worked in people's lives.

Together with her encouragement and the decision that Dave and I had made to become regular churchgoers again, my understanding of the Christian faith became enhanced. When I glanced at my beautiful daughter, in the rear-view mirror, I thought, 'How can there not be a God when this little girl of mine is so perfect?' and at that moment I accepted God fully back into my life.'

No, despite the premonition, I did not know what was waiting up ahead of me that day, but I am so grateful that I had had this 'awakening' of my faith, because I know without it I could never have even begun to rebuild my life after it was torn apart. Yes, of course, I could very well have refused again to accept anything about God and His Son, Jesus, but gut feeling made me cling to Him that day instead. Knowing if I were to endure this loss at all I would be unable to do so without His help. However, at that moment when my faith returned

43

we were still driving towards Sue's place. Before we got there, I remembered that I needed some groceries and recalled that near to Sue's street was a small supermarket where I could pick up the milk and bread required so that once we were heading home from Sue's we could go straight back.

I parked the car outside the store and then we went to get a trolley for our necessities. Lisa was so keen, I think, to see Danny that she kept running and fetching things that I needed then coming back with them to the trolley. We stopped at the stationery items as Lisa had a list of things that she would need for nursery and two of them were a school exercise notebook and pen or pencil, because on her return the children were going to be taught basic writing skills. She chose a notebook with a donkey on the front of it and I decided to buy both a pen and pencil for her to use. We made our way over to the checkout emptied the trolley and while I packed and paid I thought Lisa was still right beside me, but when I turned to take her by the hand she'd vanished. I panicked immediately and got a hollow feeling in my gut, but I need not have worried, as she had decided to be helpful by returning the trolley to the trolley-park from where we had taken it when we had come into the store. When looking back, I cannot help but wonder if that was a sign of what was just waiting for us less that an hour later, but then whether it was or not it could not have altered the outcome of that morning in Rio de Janeiro, Brazil.

Sue's house was surrounded by a fifteen foot high wall which had been painted a bright shade of white and had pantiles on the top surfaces laid in such a way that it made things difficult should intruders try to come over the top of it. The gate was made of solid wood, possibly oak, and painted dark brown. It fitted the gap in the wall perfectly and did not allow any visibility for people outside or inside to see each other. The house itself was set back from the entrance by more than twenty feet. It was also painted the same stark white as the garden walls with contrasting brown on any exposed wooden fittings and window frames.

The garden area had been reduced by about half by a swimming-pool. The pool measured approximately 40 feet by 20 feet with a shallow and deep end. Most of the plants and flowers were mature and well established. The façade of the house had climbing rosebushes attached as well as some ivy. All the plants were in various stages of bud and full bloom. It was really a beautiful setting and where we had spent many happy times with Sue, Charlie and their sons, as well as with other friends, as Sue and Charlie really enjoyed entertaining people.

The building itself was on two levels, the ground floor had a dining-room, a formal sitting room and a family room where the television was situated. The upper floor was where the bedrooms were; and also consisted of a large open veranda which had vertical wooden railings. It extended from the front to the back of the house and was

46

situated directly beneath the roof of the house. Sue used it to have social events, drinks or barbeques if the weather was wet or it was too hot to sit in the sun, it also formed a bridge over to the maid's sleeping quarters above the garage. This was a favourite place for the children to play as they could have the benefit of playing outdoors but without the danger of becoming too hot or too cold and so it did not matter what the weather happened to be. Ironically, if it had been later in the day when we arrived at Sue's, we would more than likely have had our cup of tea there instead of in the front garden where Sue chose to have it that morning. It was a truly beautiful day and I was only too willing to sit out while we could before the sun climbed high enough to take away the shade which the garden walls were providing us with.

I think it was not long after 10.00 am when we arrived at the front-gate and I rang the doorbell. There was a sudden burst of barking from inside as Sue's large dog, Ben, reacted to the sound of the bell and whoever was at the other side of his gate. I heard Sue approach the gate talking to the dog as she did so telling him to stop barking and then she opened it to allow us to enter. As we hadn't seen each other in a while we exchanged hugs and I think she made a comment about how nice Lisa looked that day and called to Danny telling him Lisa had arrived, I guess he was inside at that point.

The two little ones ran off to play inside and Sue led me over to the front patio, this was an area which was incorporated into the façade of the house which had three vaulted archways supported by stout square pillars. It was here she had the pot of tea and cups already waiting. She poured me a cup and topped hers up. All the while we were chatting and catching up on what we had been doing since the last time we were together. We could hear the children playing happily together and thought no more of it. As it was hot outside and to cool the kids down we placed a paddling-pool with water in the garden near to where we were sitting. Lisa was a bit troubled at getting into the water, I had not thought to bring a bathing-suit for her, but as she had Danny were so young I said it was okay to keep her underwear on to go into the water and it was all right to get them wet, since the sun would soon dry them and her once she had finished splashing about in the little pool. Both Sue and I had assumed that by giving them this small pool of water it would divert their attention from the larger one.

At one point Lisa came over and ask if she could have the little inflatable-ring that was lying on the table beside us. I explained to her that it was for Leon, who would need it when he came down to join us. She accepted this and went off to play with Danny again. This was the last time we talked. Leon was Sue's younger son and was born a few weeks before Kevin, and also enjoyed sleeping on in the mornings. After a short while I was getting up from my seat to go and check on what the kids were doing, but Sue said something else and I sat down again to listen and reply to the question she had just asked me. Then we heard from above our heads the familiar sound of a baby waking from sleep who was obviously hungry, so Sue went up to fetch Leon and I went to look for Danny and Lisa.

Since there wasn't any sound in the garden I went inside to see if they were there. I looked in the dining-room and then the television room. Then, all at once I heard Sue shout over and over again, 'Lisa is in the water, Lisa is in the water'. I went over and at first could not see her on the bottom of the pool's white tiled floor, and then I saw her blond hair and was frozen to the spot, glued to the ground. I realised I had to jump in and pull her out. I was just about to do this, when Sue's houseboy, Billy, a man she employed to fix things around the house and tend to the garden, suddenly appeared and seeing what had happened instantly dived into the water and brought Lisa out. At this moment I prayed to God to save my little girl. By now Sue was beside us and she began to give Lisa mouth-to-mouth but Lisa had taken in too much water, so Sue turned her over to try to get her lungs emptied, while Sue did this I kept speaking to Lisa hoping that she would hear my voice and fight for breath. When I could see how long it was taking to revive Lisa, my prayers then turned to pleading that if she were not going to survive for God to give me the strength I would need to deal with her death.

Next minute Billy took hold of Lisa, shouting in Portuguese to Sue that he was taking her to a clinic that he knew of which was round the corner that he had just remembered about. He ran with her in his arms all the way with Sue running after him. I got Danny into my car and drove to the clinic too. I can only guess that Sue had put Leon back in his cot but I don't honestly recall where he was.

The doctors tried very hard to revive my daughter but to no avail. She was dead. While the medical staff had been fighting to save Lisa, Sue phoned Charlie at the office to tell him what had happened. At this point we did not know if the

51

doctors were going to be able to wake Lisa. Now, we had to wait at the clinic for both our husbands to arrive and tell them the bad news. It was a heartbreaking task having to tell Dave that our daughter was gone and nothing could be done to alter this truth. Our precious little girl was not coming home again and so began the worst period of our lives. How were we to cope without her?

That beautiful sunny day that started out with so much contentment, a day that a mother and daughter should have enjoyed together, turned our lives into a living nightmare instead.

Now we were being driven back to our flat, I know we were taken back although I don't remember whose car we were in. I do remember walking back in through the front door and then sinking onto the sofa where I remained for most of that day, knowing what had happened but I guess utterly in disbelief. I don't think I cried, initially. All I do recall is feeling totally overwhelmed that in the few short hours that had passed since we left this same apartment together, here I was back but instead of Lisa being with me it was Dave.

Yet, once the tears did come it took many months for them to stop and years for them to stop more or less completely, but they are never really that far away.

What a difference one morning can make to a whole lifetime.

Chapter 3

How do you mend a broken heart?

In my previous book, *'One step at a time/Mourning a Child'* I wrote about the various stages and effects losing a child can have. I also gave suggestions based on what helped me to cope with some of the things most bereaved parents will come across while trying to rebuild a life without that much loved child. Through the pages of this book I want to relate what impact my loss has had on me now that thirty years have passed since that awful day when Lisa died.

Since no two children are alike, even identical twins, are completely alike; each child has a uniqueness that no one else shares. Likewise parents, both mother and father, interact differently with each of their children. This is natural and the way it should be. We are mainly governed by our own characters and traits as well as habits which we pick-up as we go through our lives. Consequently, we react to most incidents and experiences in a way which is unique to us as individuals, no matter what the situation is whether it is a good experience or not. Yes, we may laugh and cry at similar things, but we will probably not be laughing for the same reasons as our friends or the other members of the audience, because it is our natures and upbringing which trigger our funny bones. This is why when it comes to helping bereaved parents to deal with their losses; it can take a long time for them to find the solace they are seeking. Furthermore, each mother and each father may need to seek their own way of dealing with it which might be similar to their spouse's but will more than likely bring different elements to their way of coming to terms with the loss of their son or daughter. Yet knowing someone else has had a similar experience to their loss can provide a means for them to start to move forward when they feel ready to or have a desire to find their own unique coping strategies.

Through the pages of this book I intend to go deeper into the methods I used to help myself to work through the myriad of emotions and countless days of looking for ways to make things easier for me to deal with. Nothing is easy when life has dealt you the hardest blow any person can deal with, yet I was determined to survive, because I wanted my daughter's life and death to count for something and if it caused me more pain in the process so be it. If by writing I help other parents to see hope in the midst of their despair and then to seek a way for themselves to move forward then it will have been worth it and they too will come to know that once upon a time I had another daughter and her name is Lisa.

However, before I reached the time when writing became a source of release, comfort and help, we had the onerous task of contacting our families back home in Britain to tell them the news we knew was going to devastate them and the last thing they would expect to hear from us. Looking back I know I could have handled how I broke the news and whom I told differently and I have learned that I caused one of my sisters-in-law a great deal of anguish, as she was then the one who was going to have to tell everyone else the awful truth. All I knew at the time was that our families had to be told and I knew she would be at home at the time of day I decided to phone, and I have to admit something inside of me wasn't strong enough to wait until I knew my brother would be back from his work so that I could tell him, so I took the easier option, for me, and knew he would not be there but my sister-in-law would be. I am truly sorry that I did choose her to convey the news to all our other family members, but knew she would contact my brother and he would help her to contact everyone else, including both our mothers and fathers.

I honestly do not know where I got my strength from that day, but I guess because there was only Dave and I, there was no one else who could pick-up the phone to our relatives back home, it would have been much more cruel, I think, if we had asked one of our friends to do it – they had been steadily arriving throughout the day, as they learned of the tragedy – Dave did offer to make the call, but I felt that it had to be me who did it, and so I did. I made the hardest phone call I have ever had to make that day or since.

We had decided that the only place Lisa should be buried was back in Scotland and thankfully Dave's employers agreed to this request. Since, Dave was on an overseas contract this meant he could be asked to go and work in many different countries around the world, and so if Lisa was laid to rest in Brazil it would be difficult for us to leave that country, especially since our time in Rio was nearing its expected end anyway. We did not know how we would cope if we had to leave her behind in a foreign land, although, at the time, these thoughts were far from our minds. All I knew was that my intuition was telling me to take her back to our home city of Glasgow where she would be buried in our native land.

Once our choice had been agreed by Dave's employers, we could begin the process of having Lisa's body officially released and our journey out of the country approved. The Brazilian authorities had to be certain that nothing untoward had taken place and that her death was clearly the result of a tragic accident. This was confirmed at the clinic where it was established that she had died, and that no foul play had taken place. The doctors at the clinic knew this to be the case and so duly signed the papers to release Lisa's body so that she could be flown back to Scotland with us on the next plane available to Britain, once all the other official procedures had been completed.

Somebody somewhere must have been on our side; Lisa had been pronounced dead some time, I think, around noon on the 7th February 1983. We made our request to be allowed to take her back to Scotland to be buried. This was granted without delay. Soon after we had returned from the clinic we had contacted our own doctor to inform him of what had happened and he came and sat with us for most of the remainder of that day, I think he was making sure that neither of us went into shock. However, when he learned that we were planning to fly home with Lisa, he helped with the necessary procedures which needed to be set in place, making the process smoother for us. We learned that everything would be in place for us to fly out on the afternoon of Tuesday 8th February.

Reluctantly our friends began to leave but one family was very unwilling to leave and were the last ones with us. It took a bit of persuading for us to convince them that we would manage and would not do anything silly. After talking a bit more, Short, all of a sudden decided that he and his family should go. It was as if he suddenly remembered something which he had to do. We were to learn some time later that it was down to him that the following day we would see something which we never expected, but something which was like balm to our wounded hearts. After assuring them again that we would be okay, he together with his wife and daughters went home.

It wasn't till they had gone that I finally got to do what I had been longing to do ever since we had come back from the clinic, that was to go into Lisa's bedroom. I don't know why I wanted to, but I knew I needed to do it. Perhaps, that is when my tears really started to flow. Far from it being hard to step over the threshold into the room, it felt the most natural thing in the world for me to do. I just stood looking at all the things she no longer needed. For only having such a short time in the world she had amassed a lot of things. I knew without opening it that the wardrobe held clothes she had yet to wear. We had been back in Scotland only a few months earlier and I had bought her some new outfits for her to grow into, as I preferred the British styles for her outfits. Toys had been tidied, I think, but of course, Yara my home help, would have done this when she came in that morning. I sat down on the bed and just absorbed all that losing her would mean to me and her dad. Yet at the same time it felt good being in there. During the months we remained in Rio, I would go into her room occasionally and remember and cry and come back out somehow more able to face the rest of the day. I don't know why it helped me, but it did.

Although we had hoped that we could fly home on the evening of the 8th February we could not, so we would have to stay in our apartment that first night, as Lisa's body had not yet been formally released. With hindsight I am glad that we did not leave then, anyway we were not going to go anywhere without our daughter. I realised that we needed to have time by ourselves, time to cry alone and hold each other and be with Kevin who must have been totally bewildered at the goings on in our apartment that day. All the adults in his life were in tears and I do not know who attended his needs that day, I know for most of it, it wasn't me.

Yet, in amongst the searing heartbreak, there was our little son trying desperately to reach his mummy. There he was sitting with only a nappy on, on top of our coffee table. He had climbed up and the only way he could get to see me was from that vantage point, and his efforts worked. When I noticed the trouble he had gone to in order that he could see me around the 'big' people surrounding me, I could not help but smile and laugh at this little boy who knew fine well that he was not allowed to do just what he was doing at that very minute. Not only was it completely unhygienic to sit on a table, it was also dangerous for him to do this, because I feared if he fell off it he could have hurt himself. I whisked him into my arms suddenly realising I still had him and he still needed me. He was the only one who could possibly have brought a smile to my face that day and I shall always thank him for doing what he did then, making me understand that all was not lost and somehow this little boy would be the saving of me and give both Dave and me reasons to get out of bed in the mornings. Although not too early, as Kevin continued to have slow starts to his day and even now as an adult he will, if allowed to, spend most of his life lying down whether he is asleep or not.

Knowing we had a busy day ahead of us we went to bed. I put Kevin into his cot and since his room was right next to ours, we would be able to hear him if he became upset, but to be truthful I don't think he could have understood what was going on. He did know he had a sister and must have been totally confused and wondering where she had suddenly gone. When he went to bed the night before she was there, now he was up and about, but she was nowhere to be found. I do not know if anyone tried to tell him that his sister would not be home again, I know I didn't.

It was not, to my shame, until we arrived back at our apartment after the funeral in Scotland that either, Dave or I, realised that Kevin should have been more taken into account and told something about where his sister had gone. However, when I stood him on his feet on entering the apartment he ran in full of expectation and went straight to Lisa's little red table and chair and from his body language he expected to see her. It wasn't until that moment that I realised he had been missing her. The only place he connected with Lisa was our apartment, he hadn't known her to be anywhere else but there, and he would have been looking forward to playing with her, but his playmate was no longer around.

I wish I could say that from then on I was more aware of his need to know what had happened to her, but I cannot. I was lost and finding it so hard just getting myself through the day by looking after his physical and bodily needs that I had nothing left over to offer him. Yet, as time moved on I did come to understand how unfair I was being to him and strove to be more attentive to him and his need for playing and decided to take him back to his playgroup. It was not fair if he should miss out on this, too. So I picked up the phone to find out where the next session was being held and let the hostess know that I would be coming along with Kevin. I guess by this time it was about mid-April 1983.

Although our bodies and minds were crying out for rest we could not turn off the emotional roller-coaster we were on. However, we knew we had to try to have some sort of rest. I didn't know until the following day that our doctor had left some sedatives to help us relax enough to sleep, because Dave was too afraid to tell me about them in case during the night I decided the entire situation was all too much for me to cope with, and that I might prefer to join Lisa and be done with all the pain that her loss had brought me. I understood his concern, but I wish he had trusted me to want to live for him and Kevin.

After all, at that time on that night, I felt completely responsible for not being more diligent and aware of the hazard of that swimming-pool, I was the parent with her when she died so surely I was to blame for not looking after her properly and thus her life came to an end. Perhaps, it would have been the easy way out for me to take my own life, but how could I inflict even more pain on Dave and Kevin? If I were the cause of Lisa's death, then it was my duty to see that they both did not suffer even more heartbreak. No matter the cost to me I had to survive to enable them to work their way through the loss I felt totally responsible for. This was my train of thought at the onset but I have come to accept that even though I played a role in Lisa's demise, as did Sue, as perhaps did Danny, none of us were directly responsible for the decision Lisa made that day to enter the pool unsupervised and being so young she had no way of knowing what her actions would lead to and no one can know for sure why she made that decision which caused her to lose her life. Neither is she to blame for having gone into the water – it is what happens in some of our lives – and it is for those of us who are left behind to find a way of dealing with the consequences of an innocent child's choice which resulted in her death.

Chapter 4

Home for the Funeral

The next morning we were awakened by the phone ringing beside us. Dave, assuming I was asleep went through to the living-room to answer the phone there. I heard him say, 'I'll see what Betty wants to do'. He came back to tell me that his work colleague, Peter had called to say that there had been a church service arranged for us to attend if we felt able. My first thought was to refuse to go, but something made me stop before I uttered the words, 'No, I am not wanting to go,' and instead said, 'Well, it might help, so okay let's do it'. Dave went to tell Peter that we were willing to come and he replied that he and his wife Hilda would come and take us there and would be at our flat in about twenty minutes.

Peter as good as his word arrived at the time we expected him and he drove us towards the city centre. We knew that he and Hilda were Christians who attended the Pentecostal Church not far from where we worshipped in the American School in which our Catholic Mass was held each Sunday. I assumed that Peter had arranged for prayers to be said on our behalf at his church, so I was surprised that instead of turning right to go to where I knew his church to be, he turned left and drove to our place of worship. There waiting to greet us were most of the staff from Dave's office as well as friends that someone had managed to contact to inform them of this special Mass that had been arranged for us and Lisa. This was the reason for Short and his family leaving us so abruptly the night before, he had decided to set the wheels in motion to organise this gathering of people. This wonderful gesture was really appreciated by us, to think that these people had been so moved by our tragic loss, made me at least realise that we were not suffering in isolation and that these friends and colleagues were ready and willing to help if they could and in any way we wanted them to. After the service Peter and Hilda took us back to our flat where we had to pack for our long flight home.

The flying time between Brazil and Britain was at least sixteen hours plus time to refuel in Lisbon, but it might as well have been twenty-four hours or even forty-eight as to me it seemed as if it would never end. We were offered food which we could not even contemplate eating, we were offered drink which we also refused. We were even flying first class and the flight attendants could not understand why we were not making the most of all the perks we were being so freely and frequently offered. Neither were we able to sleep much.

One thing I do remember was that the in-flight movie was the first Star Wars film, I don't know why it stuck in my head, but it did. It wasn't as if I was taking in much of what was happening in the film, but I did understand that it was something to do with aliens and spaceships and somebody trying to save the Earth from some sort of invasion.

71

I realise now that the flight attendants probably hadn't been told why we were so upset and unreceptive to their hospitality. Eventually one of the flying crew came to speak to us. When he realised who we were and why we were on that flight, I figured that he did understand why we were not responding to the stewardesses' offers of hospitality which under normal circumstances we would have. This flight member must have spoken to the stewards because after this they stayed away and allowed us to be left alone, knowing now that we would ask them if and when we needed something from them. Eventually, on Wednesday the 9th February, the plane landed at Heathrow Airport.

In London we were to be met at the airport by another colleague of Dave's, Garry and his wife Sandra. They had become close friends of ours while Garry was also working in Rio, but a year or so earlier they had been transferred back to England. They had been particularly fond of Lisa. A few days after our first arrival in Rio, when we had barely unpacked, they invited the three of us to their place for dinner. We got on well instantly and chatted away as if we had known each other for some time. When it was time to eat Sandra called us over to the table where we took our seats, but when Lisa sat at her position the chair seat was so low in comparison to the table that all we could see of her was from the top of her head to the tip of her nose. Of course, Lisa didn't understand why the four adults looking at her had turned into laughing jackasses trying to suppress our laughter as we did not wish her to think that we were laughing at her, just at what she was doing. Now, here were these two valued friends greeting us in the cold starkness of an airport all of us completely bereft yet trying to stay cool, calm and together, but inwardly slowly falling apart.

They took us to have a coffee so that we could all pull ourselves together. Garry told us that our flight up to Glasgow would not be until 5 o' clock that evening and so they had arranged for us to go to a nearby hotel to wait. They had booked us a day room where we could rest, freshen-up and have some food if we needed to and they would come back to collect us and ensure that we got back to the airport in time for our flight home to Glasgow. Although we still did not feel like eating we were glad of the respite that room gave us. We were not at all looking forward to meeting our families face to face only to confirm that what we said on the phone really was true. However, we did eventually arrive back into the arms of our families and it was both harrowing and beneficial when it did happen.

One of my brothers took Dave to his parents, they were both quite frail and were not well enough to meet us at the airport and he needed to go to their home to find some comfort from them. While Dave went there my other brothers took the rest of us, in their cars, including my parents and sisters-in-law, to my mum and dad's house. When I got there more of my extended family of aunts, uncles and cousins steadily arrived to see me.

It turned out that one of my brothers had been liaising with Dave's employers about the ways and means of bringing Lisa back to Scotland and he had then gone on to arrange the funeral for her which was to take place on Friday the 11th of February; and that prayers were to be said for us and Lisa on the Thursday evening, but I cannot remember if I went to the church for the prayer service or not. I think I did because I do remember sitting chatting to some of my relatives while having some tea, but one day was simply merging into another and I was on automatic pilot doing what I was told to do and expected to do while still trying to get my brain to accept what it was struggling to acknowledge, but yet repeating over and over to myself that Lisa was dead. The next day, the day of Lisa's funeral, I know I went and I know I wore a winter coat, but I also know that I must have still been in shock. I remember arriving at the church and when I got there cousins I had not seen for years were standing with aunts and friends and automatically I started talking and joking with them as if it was just another family get-together.

They must have thought that I was going mad, for the very next thing I remember is turning around to see the car pulling up outside the church with my little daughter inside it. Lisa was so small and slight that it was decided that a hearse would be out of the question and so she arrived in her coffin which rested across the laps of Dave and my eldest brother, Billy. As this sight confronted me I kept shouting, 'No, no, no!!' Somebody, I think wrapped their arms around me and held me up while her tiny white coffin was carried into the church by Dave and Billy. I slowly followed them in and the rest of the mourners did the same behind me. I did not take in much of the service at the start, but the priest, Father Cairns, spoke so softly and tenderly and somehow he managed to catch my eye and I began to listen to what he was saying, it was then that I realised that he was speaking directly to me, or at least that is how it felt. Somehow the words he said went straight to my soul and I felt uplifted. He was explaining that because Lisa died so young and had been baptised as a baby, she had already gone to be with God in Heaven. She had been given the special Mass for someone who had died without sin called The Mass of the Innocents. We had our own special person, Lisa, sitting with Jesus, who we would be able to pray to and ask for her help.

I know that to many bereaved parents this may be a difficult concept to believe or accept, but for me it did offer me a crumb of hope when I was in total despair at the idea of a life without the one little person with whom I had spent every single day of her life. It gave me hope that since she was with God no further harm could befall her and that she was and is our treasured little angel, who God couldn't wait to have join Him. And I knew somehow in someway I would always have her in my heart if not in my life. Since then I have come to understand that wherever I am and wherever I go Lisa goes with me. She may not live in my home and we can never hug each other, but I will always have my treasured memories of times we shared and I can come together with other bereaved parents and have my special weekend with my eldest child while helping other bereaved parents do the same.

Chapter 5

Friends

Sometime after we had first arrived to reside in Rio de Janeiro in March 1980, I was informed about the International Newcomers Club (INC). This was an organisation mainly aimed at women from anywhere in the world who needed friendship in a country in which, due to their husbands' and partners' jobs, they had come to live. While Rio was on the whole a friendly city anyone coming to live there had to be aware of certain dangers which women could get into unintentionally. There were also some protocols which needed to be observed, some which in our home countries would not be a problem but could be taken the wrong way by the local inhabitants. The International Newcomers Club helped those women from English speaking countries to build a network of support while living in a country where the majority spoke Portuguese. It was open to any woman with a good command of English who wanted to make friends. If they had children they would be able to take part in the relevant toddlers' or baby group suitable for their ages.

It was through this group that I met a fellow Scot, Molly. She was married to a local man, but found that she wanted to befriend other expatriates and so she had joined the International Newcomers Club too. Her daughter's being a few months older than Lisa meant they fell into the same age bracket for their toddlers' group and that is where we met. By this time I believe she had been living in Rio for some years and although her mother visited from Scotland occasionally, Molly was very much needing to make friends with others and especially fellow Scots. She explained to me that she had little contact with anyone outside her husband's family and that apart from his mother and sisters, she had not made many friends of her own.

We hit it off from the very first time we met. It seemed to me that another problem for a woman like Molly who was married to local man was that Brazilian men were still seen very much as the head of the household and their wives were expected to 'live within the bosom of their families' or that is the impression I had. So each week at the toddlers' group we would catch up with each other's news and our friendship grew. I really appreciated her companionship and our daughters liked each other too so we started getting together at other times outwith the toddler group.

Quite near to where Molly lived was a *'Traditional British Pub'* which had an old fashioned red phone-box outside it. It served British meals like bangers and mash with Heinz baked beans, Scotch pie with chips and Bovril gravy which were so sought after by The British. The pub even had special evenings when they had taken in a stock of such items to which many expatriates from the United Kingdom came. In the afternoons the

81

pub served traditional British-style Afternoon Teas with sandwiches, scones, fine cakes and proper Indian tea served in bone china cups with saucers.

Molly had been aware of this pub long before I knew anything about it, but her husband being Brazilian could not understand her desire to taste food from her home country neither was he a great consumer of beer, at least not the type The British favoured. Thus she had not been to this pub because for women in Rio to be seen to go into a pub alone could seriously damage a woman's reputation. Neither did I feel comfortable entering a pub on my own. However, as our friendship grew we realised that there was nothing to stop us going into the pub together and that we could take our daughters for Afternoon Tea, because this would prove to any onlookers that everything was above board. We were simply having light refreshments with our little girls and not placing our morals on the line and sullying our good names.

We had a truly enjoyable time that day. We had younger sons whom we had both decided to leave at home, Kevin being looked after by Yara while she did the housework and her son, Josh who was left at home with his paternal grandmother. While it did not really matter to the girls what they were being given to eat, Molly and I relished every morsel of the sandwiches and scones and cakes and the several cups of tea that washed all of this delicious food down our throats. We had a great time. We could have sat and chatted for the rest of the afternoon, but we decided as the girls had been so well behaved it was only fair to take them to a play park which wasn't far from the pub. We had a wonderful time and before parting that day we vowed that we would do it again perhaps even once a month. Since we had each other for company and our girls got on well, there was no longer a problem for us and we could get together for another visit to the pub in future. Sadly, we were never able to do this. It was only a week or so later that Lisa drowned.

Another friend whom I met through the INC was Ellen; again she was from Glasgow, as was Molly. It was great that I now had another Scots friend I could visit anytime to stop me feeling so homesick. However, the way I met Ellen was totally different from the way I met Molly.

I had not long given birth to Kevin, I think he was about six weeks old when I felt more in need of adult company because I had not yet found the strength to get both Lisa and a new baby ready to go anywhere except for a short walk around our apartment block to a nearby newspaper kiosk. This was simply to get out of the house and see other adults even though I could not converse with them and it helped get fresh air into our lungs.

As a member of the INC each quarter I would receive by post the Newsletter. This contained useful information on where to buy certain items such as cling-film, this might be a strange item to require but in a hot country which is plagued by various types of insects, flies, ants and cockroaches, it is clear why such a simple item of food hygiene is important especially for mothers of small children. Cling-film was readily available in Rio but when you did find it, it wasn't always up to a good standard, as it either tore very easily or didn't cling to anything except itself. So we seemed to be forever looking for a brand which served the purpose it was designed to do.

Within the pages of the Newsletter there would be listed the names and contact details of more women who had either just arrived from Europe, the US or any woman who wanted to meet and make friends with other women to have socials and coffees together and so feel less isolated in a country that did not encourage friendships between neighbours and which relied upon its families to provide support and companionship. Beside the names of the women listed they would state where they came from and although I had many cherished friends of many nationalities, I had become seriously homesick and longed to hear a Scottish accent. I read down the list of the new members and there amongst them was Ellen's name. She had included in her mini-biography that she was originally from Scotland and was keen to meet any fellow Scots. Here was what I needed, but I wasn't sure how she would react to a complete stranger phoning her. I must have read her statement about six times trying to persuade myself to pick up the phone and dial the number she had given. Then I realised she could only say no and at least I would be able to welcome her to Rio. When I heard her voice at the other end of the line, I was struck dumb. The sound of her accent was like hearing a favourite tune that I hadn't heard for a long time and hearing it again brought a tear to my eye. Not only a tear came but a lump rose in my throat too. She repeated, 'Who is this?' I came to my senses and didn't want her thinking it was a crank making the phone call. So I introduced myself and explained where I lived and how great it was to hear her speak and why it meant so much to me. It turned out that she was at home minding her friends' children while the mums went out to work. This meant that she was housebound, so the only way we could spend that afternoon together was if I went to her.

Initially, I didn't think it was possible for me to get to her. Not with a new baby and a toddler who hated walking. Lisa was so used to going places in the car that even taking a walk around our apartment block was about all she would tolerate. Then I recalled that the last time we were home in the UK we had bought a baby-carrier so I could strap Kevin to my body while taking Lisa by the hand. We would be able to get to Ellen's place in a taxi; I could not go if I took Kevin in his push-chair, but so long as I was able to walk a short distance with both the children we could get to Ellen's after all. So I phoned Ellen back and told her we were on our way and should be at her door within twenty minutes and so we did. We were instantly drawn to each other and became good friends.

The way in which these two good friends, Molly and Ellen reacted to Lisa's death was strikingly different. It was hard to understand in some ways, but clear in others. Why did they react to it in such differing ways? And yet both of them were valued friends to me. Nevertheless no one can know how they will react to any given situation until and unless something happens to reveal how that person's attitudes can be so completely contradictory to another's.

After the doctors had confirmed that there was nothing more they could do for us and Lisa, Dave and I were driven back to our apartment. Of course, when we entered Kevin who had been, I think, playing with some toys came to greet us. He was delighted to see us together as normally he would not have seen Dave until the evening when he returned from work. It was the company chauffeur who drove us back but I cannot recall if he drove us in our car or the company's one. I think it must have been he who told Yara the bad news. I can't recall seeing her again that day and I figure she must have just gone home. She had been very fond of both my children and she too was heartbroken.

I think I lifted Kevin up and sat with him on my lap for a while, but those early few minutes are very vague in my mind. However, as we had no other family about us we soon realised that we had to call people back home in Scotland and start telling them this most devastating news which had torn our lives apart as it was about to do to theirs. Yet, because of the time difference we had to delay contacting them to make sure when we phoned somebody would be at home to receive the news.

Then I remembered that I was due to have coffee with Ellen that afternoon at my place. So I thought I should phone her and tell her that I wouldn't be able to meet her now. She was as friendly as usual when she answered her phone, but then I told her why I was cancelling she was stunned. Despite not being keen to drive in Rio within a short while she was at my front door having come anyway to offer me her comfort and support. She stayed with us until she had to go home to provide a meal for herself and her husband Colin. I am still grateful to her for coming to me so readily that day. As she was from our home city of Glasgow it felt almost like we having family with us and her presence helped us a great deal. It might even have been her who had made sure Kevin was fed and had his nappy changed. It certainly hadn't been me. In those first few hours I couldn't move from where I had sat down soon after returning from the clinic.

Then people kept arriving at our door, the phone rang frequently and all wanted to speak to me or Dave and I had to repeat again the scenario which took place at Sue's and the outcome of the accident. Everyone found it hard to accept and did not know what they should do, but offered to help in any way they could and that all we had to do was ask. This went on for several hours but again as we did not have other family we had little choice but to answer the phone each time it rang. I think it must have been on one of those occasions when I had just finished talking on the phone and was returning to my seat that the door bell rang and since I was right beside it I opened it. There standing with her husband was Molly. I did notice her recoil a little but I thought nothing of it. Some weeks later this simple gesture of opening my own front door was to come back to me and add to the reasons why Dave and I decided that living in Rio de Janeiro was no longer where we wanted to be, it would help to resolve in our minds that it was time that we headed home to Scotland. We would or at least I would, feel safer and be allowed to grieve in the way we chose and not have this dictated to us by well meaning and good intentioned friends. The other reasons why we left that city when we did will be included in a later chapter.

Throughout the day people would arrive and pay their respects and offering sympathy would cry or talk. I don't know why but much of what was said I absorbed. It was as if I was a sponge soaking up any crumb of comfort and advice which I might need if I were to survive this horrifying experience even if at the time I did not know whether I did want to go on or not. This thought never entered my head until several months had passed when I got to thinking that it would be perhaps an easier way out. Then I would not have to bear the endless aching of my arms to hold and cuddle Lisa as well as the unending pain which encompassed my every waking moment. Why I had the presence of mind to listen and take in what people said to me that day, I still don't understand. I don't think I took in everything, however the things I was aware of visitors saying were things like; 'my friend lost her baby to cot-death and the strain caused the couple to divorce' and 'my sister had a miscarriage but she never came to terms with it'. For some reason their words rather than hurting me or being regarded by me as mere trivial events compared to my loss, gave me the resolve to use whatever means I could to enable us as a family to emerge, not unscathed by the tragic event but despite it, somehow. Of course, I had no idea at that moment just how long a 'journey' we had begun and how hard it would be to put ideas into reality and even to sort out what reality would mean if I wanted to arrive at time when my grieving was over. Now, thirty years on, I know what I did not know then that there is no such thing as an end to parental grief.

Yet there are ways to learn to live without someone whom you had expected to outlive you; a coming to realise that nothing can ever be done to alter the facts. They have gone and they cannot come back. Does this mean forgetting them? Perhaps deciding to put their loss down to an incident that occurred, by refusing to allow time and space in our hearts and minds and 'shelve it'.

There is also the learning to live without them but wanting to keep their memories fresh in our minds and introduce them to other bereaved parents who will share their cherished reminiscences of their lost children with us, too. I have found by doing the latter that I can now laugh and joke and have a good time remembering Lisa and her funny ways while the tears are not far from my eyes knowing I shall always miss having her around. The tears of sadness now mingle with those of laughter because the love I had for her is still real and I am glad that I have shared my life with her. This is what being part of The Compassionate Friends has given me, a place where I can go and remember my daughter Lisa – to recall things we did together - talk about how I have managed to live thirty years without her - because I have found many compassionate friends who are willing to listen and want to know about her.

We come together with others who have lost children just to be together with those who understand without one word being uttered what it feels like to be in the unfortunate position of saying goodbye to our child and never to be able to share a single minute more with them here on earth. It isn't an easy thing to do to pour out you heart to strangers and I think it is safe to say that we would rather do this with another family member, but too often it is harder to find family who are willing to listen than it is to speak to a stranger over a coffee. We know how hard it is to deal with. We are doing this at first hand. We do not want them to do the grieving for us, all we do wish is that they would be willing to listen and cry with us if they want to, but all too often they turn away and refuse even to allow us to speak of our child by name. We know it hurts. All we ask is for them to sit with us and allow us to talk and share a memory or two with those who knew our child too. Instead of ignoring the subject when we mention our child's name, please share with us your knowledge of our child who was your niece or your nephew and then together we will reach a point when we can laugh together as well as cry together. It really does help us. So if anyone reading this truly wants to help support grieving parents, all you have to do is listen. Don't speak, if you don't know what to say it is better to remain silent and you will have helped far more than you will ever know. You might think that you have done nothing. However, you will have helped to share the load and given us a rare opportunity – someone who was willing to spare a few minutes so that our lifetime of heartache and longing will be just that little bit more manageable.

This is why for me The Compassionate Friends were invaluable. They do not approach bereaved parents but do make themselves known to GPs, nursing staff and other frontline organisations who are usually the first people to be called upon at the time of a child's death. This is why until the death of your child you may never have heard of The Compassionate Friends. Sadly, it is only on the death that you may need to be aware of them. Once they have been contacted they can help parents in many different ways. Most of those dealing with parents at TCF have also lost children so they know personally how parents feel and of the trauma that they are experiencing. Support and help is offered by phone contact; on line; by post; by one to one visits and/or in support groups. Parents can be linked by their locality and/or the age at which their child died or the circumstances of the death or all of these.

It depends on the individual parent how they wish to be supported. As well as these personal opportunities there are also numerous leaflets covering many aspects of child bereavement encountered by parents. These cover things like: Father's Grief; Mother's Grief; How the death may affect other family members; Dealing with the Funeral; the Police; Medical Staff; The Healing Process and many others. They have a website which is at: www.tcf.org.uk and a National Phone Helpline 0845 123 2304.

There is no right way or wrong way of dealing with the loss of your child, there is only your way. This may be totally different for each mother and father of each child as every relationship we have with another person is unique and so our coming to terms with life without them will be a unique experience too. Yet, the one thing that The Compassionate Friends provides for every parent who comes to them is a mutual understanding of the most difficult situation anyone can possibly have to deal with in the course of their life. No parent expects to outlive their child, even parents who have had a very seriously ill baby hope against medical advice that something can be done to save them from having to say goodbye to the baby they have just had.

There is an instant bond between most bereaved parents. It is invisible but very tangible all the same. Since there is no grief so hard to bear as that caused by the death of our own child, it is only another grieving parent who can fully comprehend the full impact such a loss has on us as individuals, yet this bond can somehow help each of us by the simple fact that we need not bear the burden of the loss alone and isolated from society. Knowing that others are suffering in the same way we are is both tremendously sad and at the same time it gives us hope that perhaps together we can slowly rebuild our shattered lives.

It was only after the death of Lisa that I discovered who my true friends were and who drifted away because they were unable to offer any kind of support or even a sympathetic shoulder for me to cry on. Worst still were those who could not handle it and chose to ignore me and did not allow my tragedy to darken their lives for an instant. I came to realise that Molly thought she was looking out for my best interests and that she was worried that I was heading for a nervous breakdown. While Ellen was a complete stalwart who made it clear that she would help me in any way she could, all I needed to do was ask.

It was a good few weeks after Lisa's death that I began to make a new routine for myself and Kevin. I took him to his toddler group once a week; I had resumed my weekly Mah-jongg sessions and had begun a course of lessons at Peggy's for Advanced Bridge. The INC began having evenings out for their members in which I decided to take part. Some of the events were held in various members' homes and guest speakers would be invited; for instance, one evening a Dental Practitioner came along to advise mothers on the best ways to ensure good dental habits in our children; another occasion saw a number of us including Molly going to a Chinese restaurant. These I welcomed as yet another distraction from the endless striving to work through my grief.

However, the evening I went to the 'Dental Hygiene Talk' showed me that I was still not very strong emotionally. Although the mistake wasn't mine, my lack of confidence in my decision making was severely put to the challenge. Dave had driven me to the place where the event was being held. We agreed the time for him to collect me before he headed back home with Kevin in the back of the car in his car-seat. I enjoyed the evening and it was good to have a little respite from my sadness. At the end of the evening, which had over-run slightly, I was late getting to the pick-up point where I expected Dave to be waiting. There was no sign of the car so I waited fifteen minutes, then twenty minutes passed, but when thirty minutes elapsed and still he had not come, I began to panic. I began to imagine the worst scenario that he and Kevin and been involved in a road accident, and wondered what I should do. The only thing I could think of was to go back to the house where I had been that evening and explain what had or might have happened. The dentist who had given the talk was still there and as he had to pass my apartment block on his way home he offered to take me home. My friend said she would wait where Dave had planned to collect me and let him know where I was, so I agreed to take the offer of a lift home. It turned out that Dave had fallen asleep which accounted for him not arriving when I had expected him to. Needless to say he had received a bit of a fright that evening, too, because by the time he had come to collect me I was being driven home by the dentist, but I had no way of letting Dave know where I was. Eventually, he arrived home to find me there. From then on when going out in the evening I chose to drive myself to wherever the event was being held.

Despite this blip most of my friends kept saying how well I was dealing with everything and getting on with my life. However, they didn't see me collapse in a heap onto the sofa as soon as I arrived back at my apartment, exhausted through the sheer effort it had taken to pull myself through yet another exhausting day trying to stop myself sinking into utter despair.

Unbeknown to me though, Molly had been observing my behaviour and it appeared that she thought I was behaving irrationally. I don't know how she thought I should behave, but it was not in the way I was doing so. Otherwise she would not have gone behind my back and spoken to others about me. One of them phoned Dave which set the cat among the pigeons and became another step in the process that made me decide that I no longer wished to live in Rio. It set the ball in motion which eventually saw us heading for Scotland much sooner than we had imagined.

Her concern came to a head one particular afternoon. I cannot recall where we were going, but I had arranged to collect Molly from her place and take us both to another social event. As we got into the car Molly remarked on how hot the weather was and I replied, 'Yes, I know and it is only a quarter to two'. I had only meant that since it was still fairly early in the afternoon the heat would probably rise still further. I have no idea what Molly though she heard me say, but whatever it was caused her to take the action she did and as a consequence she lost me as a friend. However, at the time I had no idea what she was about to do. So I switched on the ignition and drove us to the venue and I thought no more about that day's conversation until the following Friday evening.

Dave didn't like staying home at the weekends since Lisa died and so we were in the habit of going out for dinner or to see a movie and booking a babysitter to look after Kevin to allow us to go out. This particular Friday we were both getting ready when the phone rang. Dave answered it and after a while came to explain what the call was about. It transpired that Molly had phoned Patricia, the organiser of the INC, who had in turn phoned Sue to say how worried she was for my sanity as from what Molly had said she was given the impression that my speech was befuddled and that Molly though I needed professional help. It turned out that Molly had misheard what I had said to her two days earlier, I cannot recall what she thought I did say, but it was enough for her to cause me to become very angry indeed. Not only was I trying to deal with the loss of my daughter but now I was having to explain myself to others as to why I was choosing to do the things I was doing. This to me was nothing more than struggling to come to terms with the hardest thing any mother can be expected to deal with and now so-called friends were not allowing me to handle my situation in the way which felt right to me.

There had been others in Rio at the time who had suggested that I speak to a psychologist friend of theirs. I had thought about doing this, but I decided that I did not wish to meet with the woman and had thought I had made it clear that I knew how best to cope with my loss and what I was doing felt right to me and that they had to accept this. Molly had clearly thought otherwise and she had said on at least one occasion that she was worried that I was burying my loss instead of dealing with it. I accepted her point of view and said as much to her.

While Molly's way of trying to help me caused me more anguish than comfort. She did what she thought was the right thing to do and I guess it was better for her to seek out help on my behalf, to err on the side of caution, rather than to watch me slowly going insane. It is still important that if anyone is concerned about a friend or family member to ask them first. Before seeking advice from a health professional of what symptoms to look out for in case the person is heading for a breakdown. This may well have been what Molly had done. I just wished that she would have sat down with me and had a discussion about her concerns so that I could have given her an idea of the way I had chosen to grieve.

Ellen on the other hand had been a tower of strength to me. She would call to find out how I was. If I was down she would come and have a coffee with me and if I was okay she would chat for a little while and then leave me to get on with things. Not long after returning to Rio following the funeral in Scotland I decided that I would like to sort through Lisa's belongings. She had loads of toys which

Kevin would not need and clothes she would not need anymore and of no use to a boy. On one of the days Ellen phoned me, I asked if she would be willing to help me go through Lisa's toys and she agreed to help.

We agreed a day and time for her to come. The job was made easier because she was there. We went through everything slowly and gradually while we chatted. It wasn't as harrowing as it could have been if I had done the task alone. We sorted them into; those that Kevin could use when he got a bit older, like jigsaw-puzzles and drawing books and other such items suitable for both boys and girls; things that were suitable for a playgroup to have: these were set-aside to be donated to a local nursery that gave free spaces to children of poor families to allow their mothers to go out to work. Other items which were no longer of much use to anyone were disposed of. After two hours or so the task was complete. However, I wasn't strong enough to tackle Lisa's clothing that day as well and decided to leave those for another time.

The difference between both these cherished friends taught me a valuable lesson and that was to learn not to expect people to react to my situation in the same fashion as each other and not to expect everyone to be willing and eager to pay attention to my needs or to listen to me if I needed to talk about my situation. The sad thing was that if Molly had listened to me instead of judging me none of the upset she caused me would have happened, but she didn't and as a result we never got together again after that Friday when her concerns came to my knowledge. I did write to her a few times afterwards trying to explain why I thought what she did was wrong and why it was for me to decide how I grieved and got on with my life, whether she agreed with it or not. She never responded to these letters, so I don't know if she accepted my right to grieve for my daughter my way. I do know that she was shocked and disappointed that I had decided to leave Rio.

However, a few months after we had settled back into Inverurie again, Ellen contacted me to say that she and her husband had also left Rio and were living not far from us and we resumed our regular coffee dates the first chance we had.

Chapter 6

Time to go home

I guess we must have been back in Rio for at least a couple of weeks when I learned that I had to go to the main police station in the centre of downtown Rio. Dave told me that apparently thieves had broken into the office where my fingerprints were kept along with a batch of other peoples and this made it necessary for me to have my own redone.

As was the routine in those days of the early 1980s everyone arriving in Brazil for the first time, unless they were on holiday there, had to have an identity card and their thumb and a fingerprint recorded. This was to ensure that those coming into the country had no existing criminal record and also to enable the police authorities to act quickly in the event that you did break the law and could be dealt with if necessary as they also recorded your address. Brazil was still a Police-run country in those days so whatever they said was The Law and people were obliged to obey their rules.

Since Dave told me about batches of fingerprints being pilfered I trusted him to be telling me the truth. It turned out that this is what he told me to ensure that I went along willingly to the police station. I believe now if I had not gone there of my own freewill I would have been officially arrested and taken into custody. However I was unaware of this possibility at the time. I waited at our apartment the following morning at the arranged time for the official company chauffeur to come and drive me to the police station. Dave had told me I would be met by Winston at the entrance to what turned out also to be Rio's state prison. Winston was the company's 'gopher' he accompanied all expatriate personnel and their partners to official places where Portuguese had to be spoken and helped us to complete any official documentation we needed to keep ourselves on the right side of the Law and Order of Brazilian life.

As Dave had said he was waiting for me, I saw him at the corner of the entrance as I got out of the car. He greeted me and then turned to go into a door leading to a side room and I followed him in. It was a large room with long lines of people queuing at one side of a long counter which stretched the full length of the room and at the other side of this at various points policemen were writing things down on sheets of paper. Winston and I joined one of the queues. It took a while before we got to the front, this didn't surprise me as I had gotten used to official things taking ages to be completed. Winston gave some information to the police officer who recorded the relevant details on his sheet of paper. The police officer then led me outside and up some stairs to a smaller office. He took me inside and then told me to do whatever I was asked to do by the officers who were to take my fingerprints and then he left me there.

As I had not learned very much Portuguese I had to trust that the policemen would speak English.

They did speak enough of it to make me understand what they wanted me to do. So I pushed up my sleeves as a policeman got the ink and paper required to take my fingerprints. However, unlike when I had my prints done for my identity card where they only wanted my thumb and one finger print, this time they wanted all ten recorded. This was duly done and then I was asked to sit outside the office and wait. I wasn't told why I was to wait or why one minute I was being dealt with and next minute set aside. Neither did I have any idea where Winston was at this time. I put it down to bureaucracy and sat where I was asked to looking out on what I came to realise was the prison yard. I am glad that at the time something was preventing me from realising why I was really in this police station and that I had not twigged that there was at that moment an argument going on between Winston and a senior police official regarding whether to charge me or free me.

There was a possibility because I was the parent who was with Lisa when she drowned, even though the clinic had declared that no foul play caused her death, that I could be charged with breaking the law due to negligence for failing to be more observant and not seeing the danger that the swimming-pool presented, Dave was within his rights to have me prosecuted. It transpired, unbeknown to me, Dave was also being interviewed at the police station while I was having my fingerprints done. He told me sometime later that the policeman who dealt with him tried hard to have Dave incriminate me and have me thrown into prison; I have no doubt that would have been the death of me. It was only Dave's love for me and the sense of justice which prevented him from doing so. I believe if he had agreed to follow through with the police officers' wishes, I would not have been allowed to leave that prison alive. Because of how Brazilians feel about children I don't think I would have survived a prison sentence. Some inmate would have taken my life and seen it as just deserts for failing to be more attentive to my daughter's welfare. I don't think they would have waited to hear my side of the story. All they would know from the police was that my daughter had died while in my care and therefore it was my fault that her life ended prematurely.

During this time I was totally unaware of the real reason why I was sitting staring out at a prison yard which was surrounded by prison cells closely resembling those I had seen in the movie "Alcatraz". Had I understood what was taking place elsewhere in that building, I think, I would have become panic-stricken and I could have been charged without Dave's cooperation. If I had lost my temper and become verbally abusive towards the officers, they might have been able to charge me with offending a police officer while he was performing his duty or any other thing. I believe they wanted to imprison me that day, but thanks to Dave they had nothing to charge me with.

I do not know how long I sat there waiting and wondering, but after a while an officer came and asked me to follow him. I did as I was told not knowing where he was leading me and then I saw Winston waiting beside the door which led to the same large room we had been in earlier. We went in there and again waited our turn to be attended to at the counter, Winston did his usual talking and processing of the information the officer required him to do. As it turned out this was him having me discharged from the police's jurisdiction and even though I had no idea that I had as good as been arrested, I was now free to leave without any charges being laid against me.

Still being blissfully unaware of why I had spent all that morning in the police station I was escorted by Winston to the restaurant where I had agreed to meet Dave for lunch. As he worked nearby I had no suspicion about why he was actually in the vicinity. However, the moment his eyes spotted me the look on his face was one of sheer relief. I thought it was because I had successfully found the restaurant which I had never been to before and that he was simply happy to see me.

It was sometime later, I cannot recall how long afterwards, that I finally started to put the pieces of that day together and understood the real reason I was in that police station. I came to perceive that somehow Winston had done something which secured my release from police custody and between them Dave and Winston had secured my freedom. That day I was still unaware of how close to danger and imprisonment I had been. I sat down to enjoy a very nice lunch with my husband and as it transpired my knight in shining armour. However, once I had figured it all out this proved to be the last straw and signalled the end of our time in Brazil.

After this event when I realised how close I had come to being imprisoned as a result of Lisa's accidental drowning, I worried for my safety and my freedom while living in Rio. I was well aware of the ways the police had of applying the Law. I knew if you incurred a traffic violation they had all your details on file and would be able to track you down if you failed to pay a parking fine. When anyone purchased a car the dealers were duty-bound to send your car registration number to the police. It was then held on file. Because of the identity card system they had all the details about the car owner and the police could lay charges on a driver which must be paid should they wish to sell or trade-in the car. This meant a driver could have occurred traffic fines about which they know nothing until they try to sell their car. Then they must pay any outstanding fines before they do and if they are not in the position to pay then the amount due will be deducted from the sale of the vehicle.

Although, I had nothing to answer for, as Lisa's death was an accident with no one else involved in how her death came about, it made me concerned that if I earned a parking fine or any other minor infringement of the Law then this could be all the police would need to take me into custody again and then have all they needed to lock me up and throw away the key. This does seem a bit implausible, but in Brazil at that time the police were the Law and as such did not seem to pay much heed to a person's right to be innocent until proved guilty and since they couldn't get me for negligence of my daughter I felt they might try to get me on a minor technicality should I have as much as a minor road bump.

I remembered that after we had returned to Scotland for Lisa's funeral, Dave had received word from his employers that the company was giving us three choices on what to do once we had laid our daughter to rest. We could stay in Scotland and our belongings in Rio would be packed up and sent home to us and Dave would be found a post in one of the UK offices; we could return to Rio and complete our assignment there which was due to end within the following six to nine months, and thirdly once we had returned to Rio but found it too difficult to continue to live there we would then be allowed to go home to Scotland where Dave would be given a job in the company's Aberdeen office.

In retrospect, it would seem that remaining in Scotland would have been the easier option, but my instincts made me feel that going back to Rio would be the right thing for us to do as a family. We had left so soon after the accident that I was afraid we had left something important behind, but the truth was that had the death occurred in Glasgow or Aberdeen we would have to deal with it there and not simply run away from it. So we set the date of 31st March for returning and informed Dave's bosses of our decision. We remained in Glasgow for two weeks after this, but as we had many friends in Aberdeen and in Inverurie we felt that we would like to spend some time in the Northeast with them. One of Dave's colleagues had a flat in Aberdeen and he kindly offered to let us stay there rent free for the couple of weeks we would be in that area.

This also gave us a chance to start getting used to being without Lisa, but I am sure we were still in shock and we were simply just getting through each day the best we could.

Now that we had come back to Rio things were not settling down in the way I had hope they would, despite doing my best to set up a new routine to our days for myself and Kevin. Dave had resumed his work as soon as we had got back going out before we were awake and not returning until after six in the evenings. It was soon clear to me that my being around was upsetting other people even though I had to deal with the everyday aspect of my loss and all I wanted from those around me was to respect the way I was choosing to come to grips with it. When the scenario with the police was over I chalked it down to a procedural thing that had to be gone through to complete the accident report. When this was quickly followed on by the situation with Molly, I had had enough. It felt to me as if every move I made was under a microscope, that everything I did was being observed and it felt like I would have to be cautious about what I did and said from then on or it might be misconstrued and I would again be scrutinised and once more have to explain my actions and behaviour to others. I was not prepared to live like this and so I asked Dave to find out if the offer to ship us back to Scotland was still available. It was and so we started the process which would end our working period in Brazil.

When Molly learned that I was leaving Rio she phoned to voice her concerns, this decision to leave seemed to confirm to her that I was indeed not facing reality and that I was running away from it and now running away from Rio, too. I could understand her viewpoint. She did not want to lose me as a friend, as I believe until she met me she had been very lonely and did not have many friends to socialise with, and I know it was my welfare that drove her to behave in the way in which she did. Yet she couldn't seem to understand that I had to grieve in the way that was right for me and it was not necessarily the way in which another person would. If indeed I was shelving it instead of living through it every single minute - then this is what I had to do and one day in the future it might emerge or it may stay hidden somewhere in the back of my mind. The one thing I could not do was allow another person to dictate to me how I ought to handle the death of my own daughter. I understood part of Molly's problem was that because our two daughters were of such similar ages she may have been thinking it could so easily have been her daughter who had died. The fact is that it was not and Molly had to respect me enough to allow me to do whatever I thought I had to do in order to survive. No, it wasn't an easy choice to make to learn to survive without Lisa, but I still had Kevin and Dave and something was driving me forward whether I wished to or not. I know now that it was my faith that was leading me to somewhere up ahead and I was willing to be lead, because I could not have even got up out of bed the day after Lisa died without it giving me the strength to do so.

Once the decision had been made and it was confirmed that we could go home, I felt an instant relief. It was as if a huge weight had been moved from my shoulders and we then set about planning our journey home. It would take a couple of weeks at least to organize all that we needed to pack up and leave. There were many things to do; arranging for a shipping company to take our belongings and have them delivered by freight to Aberdeen; inform friends of our imminent departure; decide what route we would take when we left. Although on the whole it was my decision to go back to Scotland for some reason I wasn't keen to go straight back, I think I was this time delaying the inevitable heartache of returning there without Lisa, although it was a comfort knowing she was there already.

And so as we had not visited the Amazon during our time in Brazil we took the chance of leaving via Manaus, the city situated where the

Amazon and the Negro Rivers join. It was a good decision to go there and we spent a few days absorbing the smells and sights of the area and seeing these two massive rivers one black and one brown slowly merging into one great waterway. When we boarded the flight to take us to Europe our destination this time was Paris, again another delaying tactic, but we couldn't put it off indefinitely and so after a week there we boarded the plane which would finally take us home to Scotland. However, before leaving the French capital I had yet another sad episode to deal with.

I do not know and still think about why Dave asked me on the night of Lisa's death if he could have sex with me. He said he had so much tension and rage built up inside of him that he felt if he could not release it he was going to punch someone and if he did he didn't know who he would hit or how hard he would do so. As I blamed myself for Lisa's loss, I felt I had no right to say 'no' to him and if it helped him in any way to release his emotions then who was I to deny him this need. So on the night our daughter died we had sex. We did not make love; we were simply performing a primal act. No, it did nothing for me but it did allow Dave a crumb of comfort and that is the least I could do for him, having just failed in my duty as her mother to pay due care and attention to our beloved little girl.

I never told anyone about what we did that evening, but I knew I had fallen pregnant. I did not need to have this confirmed by a doctor I knew it and my body had already gone into the process it needed to for the foetus' development. I didn't even tell Dave as I didn't think he would believe me without having a doctor's confirmation, but I knew what my body was telling me and I did not need anyone else telling me what I was already aware of. Not long after we checked into the hotel in Paris I went to use the toilet expecting just to do the usual, but what came away from me was far from the normal and there was nothing I could do but flush it all away. A day or two later my body again confirmed to me that I was no longer 'with child' and we continued our next few days in Paris as if nothing had happened.

Do I feel ashamed of what I did? Well, I didn't do anything to cause that pregnancy to terminate, it happened spontaneously with no intervention by me. What may have caused it to end was flying so soon after falling pregnant but as I had not gone to a doctor for confirmation and consequently lost the embryo, I did not think an investigation would have made a difference to the result. If anything I think I was protecting us from people finding out that on the night of Lisa's death we had sex. I doubt that many people even our best friends would have understood why we could perform a 'loving act' on the same night when our whole world had come crashing down around us. So yes there was a bit of shame and a bit of self-preservation, but we were desperate parents trying desperately to find a way of coping with our loss and doing whatever it took to enable us to do this and this included having sex on the night Lisa was taken from us. And as a consequence of that action the foetus which was conceived that night, because intercourse for many months after that night just didn't happen, came to an abrupt end that week in Paris before we headed back to Aberdeen. One more thing I had to come to terms with. It was years later before I told anyone, not even Dave, about that lost baby.

As soon as we were within Scottish airspace it felt good to be home. I did not know what lay ahead of us but at least we would be on home ground and we were flying into Dyce Airport, Aberdeen. Dyce was also where Dave would be working. Even though our families lived several miles to the south in Glasgow, it felt good that we would be much nearer to them and could visit them whenever we wanted to; instead of being thousands of miles away from them when even to phone them cost a lot of money. And yet they would be far enough away for us to be able to continue our grieving at our own pace and not have more people telling us how we should or should not deal with it. The overwhelming feeling I had was 'at last we are home' and it felt good and it felt right; and I knew our decision to come home was the right one for all of us. When I fell pregnant later that year is when I admitted to the gynaecologist about the spontaneously terminated embryo.

Chapter 7

Inverurie

It didn't take us long to find our new home and once again our preferred choice of where to buy it was in the Aberdeenshire town of Inverurie. This is where we had lived before moving to Rio de Janeiro and I still had friends there. It was also where Lisa had spent most of her life and as we had enjoyed living there in the past it felt like we were returning home, even though our time there had been tainted with an unhappy event.

Lisa had been born on 7th November 1979 and although we abstained from intercourse for the six week period which was the medically recommended time after giving birth and I was breastfeeding Lisa, I had been told that this would act as a natural contraceptive and so I shouldn't become pregnant while I still fed her myself. However, by the following November I knew that I was once more expecting a baby. We accepted since it was our fault for not taking adequate precautions to prevent another pregnancy that we would welcome this new life with open arms. Not to be, alas.

We had come down from Inverurie to Glasgow to spend Christmas with our folks and we were staying at Dave's mum and dad's place in Bearsden which is near Glasgow. We had all had an enjoyable time. Then after going to bed as normal, in the early hours of 27th December, I was wakened very abruptly to discover blood was flowing from me profusely. I had started to haemorrhage very badly and was taken to the hospital by ambulance. There was nothing they could do. I had lost too much blood and my body had begun to reject the pregnancy. I was devastated as were both our families. I was told that 'these things happen' and that 'It was nature's way of dealing with an unhealthy embryo' and that 'Once your body has recovered there will be no reason why you should not try for another baby and have a more positive result'. Although I understood these words were intended to comfort me they didn't and I felt heartbroken.

I never have grieved properly for that foetus for even though to me it was a baby and my body had begun preparing for it – now I was being told it was my own body that had identified something wrong with the development of the embryo and so nature had caused it to be aborted. Readers might be interested to know that this is the first time I have written about this lost baby as I did what others had told me to do and accepted that miscarriages were nature's way. I accepted the situation as I was told I should and then got on with looking after my daughter and try to be a good mother to her. This was another reason that when I went on to suffer the loss of Lisa I was determined that she too would not become 'just another statistic in the course of my life'. If I could help others come to terms with their own tragic losses then Lisa's life and death would count for something and she would not be forgotten.

When we had the chance to return to Aberdeenshire, Inverurie was the only place were I felt I would be able to learn to live without her, in my own time and in my own way. Dave had chosen his way by shutting it all out. I know he hasn't forgotten her or how she died, but he refuses to talk about her loss and just gets on with living. Sometimes I wish I could do the same. I can't and I have to be strong enough to allow him to grieve in his way, because I demand the same respect for myself. Yes, it hurts that I have to go to other people when I need to recall the things I did with Lisa, but that's the way it has to be. I do hope one day that Dave will open up and allow in the happy memories, but I think to do so, he has to allow some of the more difficult and painful emotions to emerge and I think this is what he is still shielding himself against.

Inverurie was also convenient for Dave as it was only a twenty minute drive to his place of work in Dyce, which is a suburb of the City of Aberdeen. Dyce is also where the airport is situated yet another advantage to living in Inverurie as very often Dave would need to fly to London or other places around the world in the course of his job. For us as a family it was the best town to serve all of our needs. We moved into our new home in June 1983.

The day we were moving in Dave had to go to work so I was left with the task of seeing that the removal men put items where they needed to be. While the men off-loaded our belongings from their van into the house one of our new neighbours kindly invited Kevin and I for coffee and a chat. So once I had informed the men what furniture should go into which room, I went with Kevin to the neighbour's house. From that day we got on very well with her and the other neighbours who were all very friendly and we were made to feel as if we had always been there and not just moved in. There was a baby-sitting circle organised by the mums and I was invited to come to their next get together, where I met the other mums on the rota and decided to add my name to the list of babysitters.

All was going well so I decided not to reveal my recent history to them in regards to Lisa's loss. How do you go about introducing a subject that you feel might throw a wet blanket over new found friendships? Neither was I going to deny my loss, but there hadn't been a convenient moment in which to mention it so I didn't. I think it was about four or five weeks after we moved in that the topic surfaced. Since we moved in during the schools summer break many of the neighbours' children were around during the day. One of them would often come in and play with Kevin. She was a very curious girl but I didn't mind answering her questions. One morning she noticed one of the family photographs on a shelf and asked who the little girl was. As she wasn't too young to understand and was quite mature for her age I decided to be honest with her and told her that it was a picture of my daughter, Lisa, and that she had drowned.

Of course, the young girl was surprised and asked why I had not said anything about her before. To this question I replied, 'The right time to mention it hadn't arisen, until now'. I realised that I should now go and let the girl's mother know about Lisa in case later on her daughter became upset by what I had told her. I hadn't gone into details of how Lisa died, simply that she'd gone into the water and by the time we found her it was too late to save her, which was true. I wanted to give the young girl an awareness of the possible risk of swimming-pools, but I didn't want to scare her completely, but I still thought I should speak to her mother. Again the neighbours were very kind and sympathetic, even though they were obviously taken aback when I told them of Lisa's death, but I let them know that my loss was not a secret and that I didn't mind others knowing about it. It sort of felt like a weight had been lifted off my shoulders and now I could get on with the task of trying to rebuild my life, in my way and in my own time.

There was another incident which arose through me trying to protect Dave as well as others from having their evening spoiled by revealing the death of Lisa which I imagined would put a damper on everyone's enjoyment. I was the only one who hadn't enjoyed the occasion, because by the end of the evening I was the one laden with guilt while the rest of the company there carried on with their evening unaware of my torment.

Dave and I had joined other colleagues of his for a dinner party at a hotel in Aberdeen. This was the first such social we had attended since arriving back from Brazil so I didn't know who among Dave's office colleagues knew about our situation. I thought one or two would know, but since Dave didn't like talking about it, I decided not to say anything. This was very hard for me to do, because as soon as people know you have children they want to know how many you have, if you have two or if you intend having another if you have one. To the question of how many children I had, I said simply that we had a son and left it at that.

However, later on when we were sitting eating the man sitting near to me started speaking about his sister and how she had one child with another on the way. He was wondering how the older one would react when the new baby arrived. Without thinking about it I started offering some tips on how I got round this when I had to introduce Kevin to Lisa. I was careful not to say why I knew what to do and why I knew my tips had worked, trying not to say that I had learned these methods by trial and error so knew what worked and what didn't. I was praying that this man would stop his probing as I was becoming annoyed, not at him but with myself for having not stated at the beginning of the evening the truth about once having a daughter called Lisa, who sadly had died. Eventually, I think somebody managed to change the subject and for the rest of the meal I remained silent.

As a result of this event I resolved that from then on I would always mention Lisa when in company. If people wanted to know more about her or our loss then I would tell them. If they didn't wish to know they would change the subject or pretend they hadn't heard me this was alright with me too, because at least I hadn't betrayed the memory of my daughter just because it made others feel uncomfortable.

For most of our time in Inverurie we were able to grieve at our own pace, taking each day at a time. If I didn't feel like going out Kevin and I stayed home and pottered about the house. At that time daytime television had not long begun and I found this to be a great escape. It gave me a distraction and helped pass some of the day. However, this was not fair on Kevin and while the school pupils were still on holiday he had plenty of people older and younger and of his own age who would play with him outside or if it was raining in our house or some other mother's home. But when they returned to school I knew Kevin would not have the same amount of pals around and those of his own age would either be at nursery or playgroup. So I had to pull myself together and get out and about for his sake.

In the town's community centre there was a Mothers' and Toddlers' group which met three times a week Tuesday through to Thursday, so we started going there. I also learned that the local high school offered evening classes during term time and one of the courses on offer was Secretarial Studies which included typing lessons. There I could pickup the skills needed to turn my handwritten manuscript into a format suitable for sending to an editor of a publishing house. So I signed up for these.

Slowly, I was getting into a nice routine and Kevin seemed to be none the worse for our abrupt move from a near tropical climate to the very changeable weather in the northeast of Scotland. I had also become very involved with my local parish church and attended many of their organized groups. I became a parish councillor, went to the Discussion and Liturgy Groups which chose relevant hymns to be used at the next four to six services. Whenever a new group was being set-up or considered there I would be offering to help. On the evenings that I wasn't out at one of these meetings, which could mean I was out three or more evenings each week, I sat up late doing crosswords and wordsearch puzzles and anything else to occupy the small hours and prevent me going to bed.

Eventually, Dave complained that I seemed to be deliberately avoiding having time alone with him. To some degree he was right. The last thing I wanted to do was 'make love' when my emotions were already used up just trying to keep myself from sinking into a quagmire of despair. I felt that if occasionally I could get into bed and have Dave just hold me in his arms for a little while without any sexual intent, and then I would have been more compliant and mindful of his wishes. As each month passed I became aware of how selfish I was being. We reached a compromise which suited us both, I gave up some of my evenings out and went to bed at about the same time as Dave and if anything happened we would let it run its natural course. If I was not feeling like taking it further then he would have to accept this to be the case. From then our relationship began improving again.

Kevin really enjoyed his time at the toddlers group. It was run on an unstructured format. It was held in a large room with many varied toys suitable for babies just finding their feet through to boisterous boys and active little girls. It was a safe environment for children to play with larger toys and equipment our homes did not have the space for such as ride on tractors with trailers and wooden climbing-frames. All the children loved the size of the room where the mums sat along one side of the room chatting while keeping an eye and ear on the children and intervening only if a little dispute threatened to come to blows or if their child hurt himself in some way.

One day when we were walking along the street on our way home with another mum, Jill, and her four year old son. She told me that as her son was due to start school the following term, she had been doing a course at the high school and she was planning to do part time work when she had more time. Until then she was going to be looking for some typing work that she could do at home. She had heard that university students needed their work typed before handing in their essays to their lecturers and there was good money to be earned from doing this. This she felt would help to build up her confidence as well as her typing speed for when she did apply for secretarial jobs in a few months time.

My evening classes had been disrupted when Dave's father died suddenly. He died from a form of pneumonia six months after Lisa's death. So my typing course had to be halted while I dealt with the after effects of yet more heartache for our family and helped to support Dave, who now had to cope with the loss of his Dad on top of Lisa's loss. Because of this and other reasons I knew I was getting nowhere fast with my typing.

When Jill spoke about taking in freelance typing work I asked her if she would consider taking on the task of turning my handwritten manuscript into a typed one she agreed with me paying her for the work and time she spent on it. At last it was in a presentable condition to start offering it out for publication. This lady helped me greatly by enabling me to do this. The saddest part of this particular part of my story is that Jill too became a bereaved parent when her son died very suddenly due to a very virulent form of meningitis. This happened many years later when the boy was in his early teens.

Yes, there was a time when I felt cursed and whoever I came in contact with or got to know in any way would also suffer from some kind of tragedy. I know how irrational this thinking was, but my confidence wasn't that great at the best of times and I felt like a Jonah bringing bad hexes to the people I befriended. This feeling was strengthened when soon after returning to Inverurie another friend of mine who also went to the same Mothers' and Toddlers' group on the same days as us with her daughter, told me that her little girl had been identified as having cystic fibrosis. This is a terminal condition and usually results in death by the child's teens although on occasions they can live to be a bit older. Their longevity depends on their ability to deal with their condition and medical support to help prolong their lives for as long as possible. Death seems to be inevitable unless the person can have a transplant before their body becomes too damaged by the condition which slowly robs them of the ability to breathe properly. My friend's daughter lived until March 2003. After a long struggle, but with many good years in-between, her body became too weak to continue.

For a long time, it felt to me, that I was the common factor in all these peoples' lives and somehow I was the cause of their tragedies. I know that this is not the case and these things would have happened anyway whether I knew these women or not, but at that time my self-confidence was pretty low and these events were not helping me to feel any better about myself.

Sometimes I thought I was doing alright despite the loss of Lisa, and I would begin feeling better but at others I would feel my mood deteriorating and I would become morose and weepy. It took me a while to realise that this was another symptom of my grief. One afternoon - I think it would have been a Friday because I don't remember being out that day I had put Kevin down for his nap and sat down on the couch to watch the BBC's lunchtime programme, Pebble Mill at One. I watched this most days as I found their features interesting and it gave me something to do while Kevin slept. This particular day they were talking to two women who were being interviewed about an organisation they were both involved with called The Compassionate Friends (TCF).

It was a self-help support group of bereaved parents offering help and comfort to other parents needing understanding from others who had also had a similar tragedy in their lives. I listened with added interest of course and at the end of the programme I jotted down the contact details for viewers. Although I knew I was coping as well as I could with my loss and did not feel a need to seek support for me, I thought it would be useful to have the address in the event somebody else might want to contact them for help. It was a few weeks later that I decided since I had been coping well, or so I believed, that perhaps I could offer to become a helper and offer my support to other bereaved parents. I wrote off to the head office in Bristol and that was the start of my involvement with them and I have been supporting bereaved parents while having my needs met at the same time from helping them, for most of the time since.

I didn't know that still more heartbreak was waiting to trip me up. We did not plan to add to our family nor did we take steps to prevent me becoming pregnant. So it was with mixed feelings that in late November 1983 I discovered that I had conceived on one of the few evenings we had had intercourse since we had settled in Inverurie. Although the pregnancy seemed to progressing well enough, one day at the toddlers' group when I went to the toilet there was a show of red on my underwear. I knew of a friend who was a nurse and decided to call in on her on my way home as I had to pass her house on the way up the road. When I told her what I discovered on my under garments, she would not let me leave her place before I phoned Dave and arranged for him to come home early from work to collect me from her place and take me to our house in the car and then to arrange for an emergency doctor to come and examine me.

It turned out that the baby had stopped growing and I had to be admitted to the hospital to find out why. After being examined in the ward the doctor told me that the baby had died in the womb and they would have to remove the foetus from my womb otherwise my body would have to expel it. This would mean going into labour to deliver a dead baby. I decided to allow the doctors to perform a dilatation and curettage (D & C), which would clear out my womb. The day they performed the procedure was almost a year to the day since Lisa had died. Just a year before I had lost my little girl and now I was losing the baby I hoped would help me to deal with her death.

The sad thing was that Dave didn't realise he wanted more children until I had lost that baby. I was never told the sex of the baby as I think I was too traumatised at yet more loss. Not only did I feel I had been a lousy mother to Lisa, now I couldn't even carry a baby in my womb, this being the second one I had lost since Lisa's death. Within the space of a year I had lost a toddler and two unborn babies I wasn't prepared to risk putting myself through the mill again and told Dave that my body would have to have time to recover fully before attempting to have another baby and that he would have to be patient until I felt that I could risk yet another failure. At least, we still had Kevin and if he was to remain an only child then that is the way it had to be.

After some months had gone by and my menstrual cycle had returned to its normal pattern, I agreed to let nature take its course, not that we were having sex very often. Consequently by the June of 1984 I was pregnant again, this time it progressed normally but the due date I was given was the 7th February 1985. Lisa had past away on 7th February two years earlier. I prayed that the baby would come earlier than the given date and he did. Our son, Marc, made his appearance on the morning of 2nd February, a bit low in weight but with no complications.

I was glad he was a boy as I wasn't sure if I was ready to welcome another girl into my heart yet. Now we had a little boy to become a playmate for Kevin. Life began to settle down, we had two sons now and as we thought we'd be in Inverurie for a while we decided to get a puppy for the boys to help rear, and so 'Floppy', a Springer spaniel came to join our household.

Our lives were soon to be disrupted yet again when Dave received word that he was to be transferred to work in the company's London office which meant packing up everything again and starting to house hunt this time in Essex where we had chosen to live, since it was within reasonable commuting distance by train for Dave's office. We bought a house in Colchester, unpacked and began to settle down once more.

Chapter 8

Steps towards publication

As I had been very involved with The Compassionate Friends while I lived in Inverurie and had become the County Contact for Aberdeenshire, I let them know that I had moved to Colchester and asked if there was a group or contacts near me. I was sent a list of bereaved parents' addresses within my vicinity but none of them were the main contact although some had expressed the need for a group to be set-up. I got in touch with each of them to find out if they were still interested in forming such a group and enough said yes they would. We began by meeting in one another's homes.

We did enjoy our time in Colchester. By this time I had become more proficient at typing and had a basic computer and printer and was trying other ways of breaking into the 'writers' sphere'. I found that the local college was running a Creative Writing Course and although my story was far from fiction, I thought at least I would be among writers and they might have ideas as to where I could find an appropriate outlet to send my manuscript. I got a lot out of that course and again my confidence grew but I still did not find a publisher for my book. I did enjoy trying other kinds of writing such as Short Stories; and various styles of poetry, such as haiku and free verse.

We had really started to make a good life for ourselves and meeting with other bereaved parents was giving me the outlet I needed to help me with the ongoing struggle of living without Lisa. I was discovering it did not matter how many distractions I employed to occupy my mind, I was still a long way from fully accepting her loss and the longing within my heart for her continued.

We were soon on the move again, this time we were heading back to Glasgow. Dave and I had not lived in our home city for a period of ten years

153

which had taken us to Aberdeen, Rio, back to Aberdeen, then to Colchester and at last we were being transferred to the company's Glasgow base. Any other time we would have welcomed going back and in many ways we did, but we had to uproot our two boys yet again and I had to leave more friends behind and try to make new ones once more. However, this move was to have a hidden blessing which I had to find for myself. It made me feel at last that I could really call myself a writer. I could believe I was one instead of feeling that I was playing at it. My ambition to have my story put into print had progressed, but I was still a long way off.

This time we chose to buy a house in the Renfrewshire town of Erskine. There were a lot of new houses being built there and we did not want to get involved in a chain or a bidding war, so we choose a brand new build that would be completed in time for us to transfer our things from the South East of England to the West of Scotland. Moving houses for the third time within a period of about four years didn't seem to faze the boys who adapted surprisingly well to their new home. We had chosen to move towards the end of the school year so that Kevin could have a chance to meet the pupils he would share a class with but not so near the end of term as to be not worth enrolling into the school until the start of the new school year.

With Kevin at school the next task was to find things for Marc and me to do. I soon found a toddlers' group for Marc, but this time instead of my having to remain in the building I was able to take him there and leave him for the two hour session if I wished. However, as I was keen to get to know local women and hopefully make new friends I chose to stay most days to have a coffee in the parents' room and chat to the other mothers who did the same.

Then I got to know about another group called "Open Door". This was an outreach programme set-up by the Social Work and Education Depts. of Renfrewshire Council to

155

prepare women for returning to work after having their children. This organisation ran training courses in a wide range of topics, a number of different vocational opportunities for further education and other ways for women to build up their skills and eventually have the confidence to apply for and secure jobs after being at home to raise their children. As Marc's Toddlers Group only took place a couple of times a week I would also take him to the Open Door meetings which were held in part of a primary school. Here they had a large room with supervision for the youngsters and a separate narrower room where the mothers could chat and have a coffee and where invited Speakers would give a talk on their particular field of interest.

It was while I attended this that I learned that there was to be an Open Day at the local library to highlight the new courses being offered for the next school term. The courses ran concurrently with the schools hours so it enabled mothers to attend classes without worrying about being home for their kids and it also saved the expense of hiring a child-minder while improving their employment skills. I decided to go along to this, as when Marc started Nursery School I would have more time on my hands.

Meantime I had continued to send my manuscript to publishers. Sometimes it came straight back as if it hadn't even been taken out of the envelope; other times I had clearly sent it to the wrong genre or publishing house. However enough editors had added comments that gave me hope that it was only a matter of time before it landed on the right editor's desk. As I hoped to find a Writing Course to attend, I went along to the Open Day not expecting to find what I was really looking for, but thinking I might find a course that would help fill in the time while the boys were out doing their own things.

When I entered there were a few women milling about, some at notice-boards which were arranged around the room and others looking at the leaflets and information handouts lying on various tables. The organiser, a very astute lady, Betty Hemphill, could see that I was looking for something but had not found anything which appealed to me. She came over and spoke to me. 'Can I help you? Is there nothing here that takes your fancy?' I turned to speak to her and said, 'Not really'. So she asked me what had I hoped to find and I explained, 'Anything to do with writing. Like a Creative Writing Course or a Writers' Group'. She was very interested in this, took my contact details and promised to be in touch, as she had to speak to some others first.

A few weeks later I answered the phone and discovered it was Betty Hemphill at the other end of the line. She had spoken to other women she knew who had also expressed an interest in writing. Some of them had done a Creative Writing Course and were now keen to meet with others to take forward what they had learned on that course. Now, she was calling me to inform me that some of these women had agreed to meet at the local Community Centre in Erskine. She gave me the date and time and I said I would like to come. That meeting was the start of the Erskine Writers Workshop which has gone on to produce many successes and led a few of their novice writers into the publishing world. It is also where I really began to think of writing as a possible career. Still my quest was focussed on one thing. If becoming more involved with writing as a job or a means of passing the time while the boys were not at home might also enable me to find a publisher for my story then so be it.

I never set out to be a well known writer only to do anything I could to help other bereaved parents but if this meant learning all I had to learn about how to put words on to paper in such a way that someone would want to buy what I had written then I was willing to walk that road. However, if it led to fulfilling my longing to tell people about the beautiful daughter I once had the privilege of caring for that would be a bonus.

At the time of that first meeting I did not know that I was soon to become the mother of another equally beautiful daughter, Fiona. So when the same group of women convened for our next meeting at the beginning of the new school year I was heavily pregnant. As I was a founder member of the writing group, when she was born, Fiona became an honorary member of the Erskine Writers Workshop.

Now, I had two sons and a daughter to care for, but we no longer had our dog, Floppy. While living in Colchester Marc had become more active as children do as they grow, but the dog appeared to becoming too possessive of me and twice he had put his jaws around Marc's wrist. The dog didn't actually bite him, but I decided it was too big a risk and that it might one day bite him for real, so I decided to find a new owner for Floppy, one that did not have small children and so we had to part company with him. His new owner was in training to be a boxer and did a lot of running for exercise, something which I couldn't do with two small boys to take care of, so I knew the dog would be better off with him.

Life was settling down nicely and we were all enjoying having family close at hand and being able to visit them anytime we wished. This was not to last and after nearly five years we heard that again we were being uprooted and once again heading to Aberdeenshire. There was only one place I was willing to live and did not even consider anywhere else but Inverurie. In 1993, we again packed up everything and set off for our next house. This time, though, I was going to make sure that this would be our last upheaval. The children needed stability and to make friends that they could keep instead of starting over again and again.

While we had lived in Erskine I had not informed The Compassionate Friends where I had moved. I decided that I would try to 'go it alone' to see how things would work out and on the whole everything went well. However, I did eventually let them know that while I would be willing to support parents on a one to one basis I did not wish to be the main contact for that area.

During this time in Erskine I really thought that I was doing well, but I didn't realize that I was heading for a deep bout of clinical depression. I had been referred to a consultant because I had repeated occasions when I had to have anti-depressant tablets prescribed. I was still coping with the bereavement and perhaps by that time I had thought I should have come to terms with it. It took me a while longer to come to the understand that child loss is something a parent never truly gets over but eventually learns to live with it on a day to day basis and the missing and the longing for what can never be continue as long as the parent lives. I knew that the depression was not directly brought on by the loss of Lisa, but perhaps by trying to put it behind me sooner than was good for me and by no longer meeting with other bereaved parents I was not being given the opportunities I needed to talk about her and her loss with people who understood the depth of emotions experienced.

Again we opted to buy a new house rather than get involved in a chain or put in a bid for a more established property. We moved into our new home in April 1993, and live there still, this being the longest we have ever lived anywhere throughout our married lives; we have *at the time of writing been in this house more than 19 years* and I for one have no intentions of moving to another house ever again. The boys settled into their new school quite easily and I found a playgroup where Fiona, who was three years old, could go for a few hours most days.

However, this time Inverurie did not work its 'magic' for me and I sank further and further into depression and it manifested itself by causing me endless, sleepless nights. I reached a point where if I did not get even one night's unbroken sleep, I was in danger of doing real harm to myself. My doctor prescribed Prozac but this only made me hallucinate.

I told her if I could not get a sleep soon then I felt that I would walk out in front of a bus. This was when she recommended I check myself into Cornhill Hospital, the hospital in Aberdeen for those suffering from a mental illness. At that point I would have gone anywhere so long as I was promised a good night's sleep. I spent most of the month of June 1994 in the Buchan Ward of that hospital and yes I did have several good nights' sleep. I was able to reassess my life thus far and realised that the source of my depression was that I had lost confidence in myself as a mother and felt very inadequate as a person.

Spending that time away from my children, though Dave brought them into the hospital each night to see me, was both difficult and necessary. I had at no time become a threat to them, only to myself, but I think I just needed 'time-out'. After all for the past eleven years, up until that point, I had been on a roller-coaster ride of emotions; moving homes; making friends only to leave them behind;

miscarriages while still trying to deal with the loss of Lisa. Is it any wonder I crashed? I look back on that time in hospital as the saving of me. I met some lovely people in that ward, one who is and will always be a trusted friend of mine and who myself and my family hold very dear to our hearts.

When I was discharged from the hospital I came out without needing any drugs other than six or seven sleeping pills, to take if I became concerned again about not being able to sleep at night. They were there just as a safety measure if things started to get on top of me again. I did eventually use them, but only occasionally and once they were finished I never asked for more feeling confident in myself once more to be able to fall asleep unaided.

I resumed my quest to find a publisher to take on my story. Many people, I know, felt that I was struggling in vain and that I should give up on my quest, but stubbornly I refused to give up. I believed there was a market for a book like mine and continued to persevere with my task. All the time I was gathering more skills and 'know-how' and trying various other ways to break into writing, sending work out and having some small successes along the way. Then in 1996 the Dunblane Massacre shook not only Scotland but most of the civilised world too, when so many little children and their teacher were gunned down in their school.

This made me finally take the matter into my own hands. I decided if no one was prepared to take a chance on my book then I would self-publish it instead, so I did. And in 1997 it was published as, '*Sowing the Seeds of Hope/Coping with Child Bereavement*'. I was not surprised when it started flying off the shelves. However, I had no support association and did not know how best to take the book to a wider market outside of Scotland. So after a year of trying to decide what to do with it, I sent a copy of it to Floris Books of Edinburgh and they decided to take it on. So in 2001, '*One step at a time/Mourning a Child*' was published. I had at last achieved what I had set out to do. It had taken nearly twenty years to do so but it had finally happened. A book that would help others people find their own way of dealing with the loss of their own child and in their own time.

Chapter 9

A Long Slow Learning Curve

After thirty years of being a grieving parent, have I completed the journey? Would I have done anything differently? Would I go back if I could and erase the past heartbreaking years? These are some of the questions I ask myself and have thought a lot about often, not only because of this milestone marking the 30 years since February 1983. I think the best way to answer these questions is to take one at a time and answer them the best I can.

Has my journey through grief finished?

In some ways, yes it has. I have found ways of dealing with the aftermath of emotions as I have told in earlier chapters. However, I can't honestly say that I will never ever again feel as I did when I became a bereaved parent all those years ago. When I think of the person I was then and am now – they are two very different people. Am I glad about this? I would be lying if I said I wasn't. I am surprised that I was able to want to live on without Lisa to care for and would never have envisaged the journey I would take while I was adjusting to not having her around. It was only after I accepted that all my longing and wishful thinking was not going to result in her coming home to me ever again that I decided to try to live the best way I could – for the sake of Lisa.

I didn't want people to look at me years down the line and say, 'the poor thing never got over the loss of her little girl. Look how wretched she has become'. No, I wanted them to look at me and say, 'I can't believe she is a bereaved mother. Look at what she has been able to achieve despite her broken heart'. This is not to say that I am glad that I became a grieving mother, I wouldn't want my worst enemy to have to endure the pain this inflicts on the sufferer of such a tragedy, rather that when I turned to God in prayer and asked for His help, I was given the ability to rebuild my life. Through my writing I was given the means and then inspired to seek ways to use what I have written for the benefit of others.

Is my journey through my grief completed?

Largely yes, because I have accepted that no one can alter the past and nothing can bring Lisa back. On the other hand I am still her mother and the love I have for her still exists within me, so I shall always miss her and wish my life had not been blighted by her death. Yet nothing can erase the time we did share together, I realise that any reader whose child was even younger than Lisa at the time of her death might find this a hard passage to deal with. I am sorry if my words offend you in anyway, but I have to be true to the way I had to deal with my loss. I do offer you my sincere condolences for the very short time you had with your babies at whatever age they died. The truth is I don't think it is possible to feel that the 'journey' through grief for a bereaved parent is ever over. The best we can hope for is that we arrive at a time when we enjoy recalling happy, fun times we shared with them. We should try to live the best we can. It might not be that great, but we should strive to do this anyway even if it is just to enable us to face yet another day without our beloved child.

Would I have done anything differently?

I could say that I wished that I had never lifted the phone receiver that morning of 7th February 1983. I could say that if we had stayed home that day Lisa might still be alive today. I could say that perhaps if I had known that there was a supply of sedatives in the apartment on the night of the tragedy I might have taken enough of them to ensure I didn't wake up to face the ongoing nightmare I had to endure. I could even say that had we not gone to Brazil and enjoyed our time in Rio, then our family might have remained intact and not been ripped apart so violently that sunny Monday morning under a clear blue sky.

However, I did answer the persistently ringing telephone and I did set out to spend a morning with friends along with Lisa, blissfully unaware of how that day would unfold. I've then forever more had to learn to live with the consequences of that simple act of replying to a phone call which my first instinct was to ignore. Of course, I regret what happened that day and wish things could have turned out otherwise, but it didn't and therefore the only thing left for me was to pick up the pieces of my shattered live and limp on the best way I could for the sake of Kevin and Dave as well as Lisa.

Through the years of grieving the most fundamental aspect I learned from the whole experience was that – every single parent of each lost child has to find their own unique way of coming to terms with this most tragic of losses. Yes, there are parents who seem to be able to put their child's death behind them relatively quickly. Putting it down to, perhaps as we have heard time and again, 'just one of those things'. And they are able to move on from it relatively unaffected. If this is the only way they are able to deal with their loss then other people, including other bereaved parents, have to respect their right to do this. It doesn't mean they did not love their child in the same way or to the same degree as we love our deceased child; it is their way of coping. Many other parents have found help through organisations like The Compassionate Friends. Other groups exist to support parents whose children have died from terminal illness, for those whose babies died from cot-death, stillborn or neo-natal, and many others all offering grieving parents a place of understanding and comfort.

Personally helping support other parents was my only outlet. I knew that my Christian faith was my main source of comfort and gave me the strength to move forward each new day and strive to achieve my goal. In turn this gave me another reason to get out of the house and prevented me from moping around and allowing self-pity to bring my mood down even further.

However, I learned that by making myself available to other parents in my situation whose children had died from whatever cause, I was also given a chance to talk about Lisa and how her death had impacted on my life; and to share with others strategies which helped me get through another day of dealing with other people's reactions to my loss.

Especially helpful is discussing with them the problem with close family members, who at the sound of our child's name or if we wanted to talk about their loss would turn away or pretend they didn't hear us or change the subject instantly. Talking about this helps us to realise that the problem is not ours. It is our family's inability to understand that talking about our child is the best possible way of helping us. It helps us to keep the child alive in our memories. The memories are all that still remain of them, after all, and we ache to share them with people who also knew our lost child.

When our brothers, sisters, cousins and even our own mothers and fathers carry on with their lives as before as if our child had never existed let alone just been buried, this only serves to deepen our pain. It is extremely upsetting when those who knew our child almost as well as we did will not allow us to talk to them of how we are feeling about our loss. When they will not share memories of our children with us which would help us to hold on to our children in some small but tangible way their attitudes only anger and upset us adding insult to injury. This can cause fractures within the wider family that may never be mended.

This is one thing I would like to have done differently would be to have explained to my extended family that it helped me if they allowed me to talk to them about Lisa. Not necessarily about her death but just to share a memory or two of times when we had laughed at some of the little amusing things that toddlers tend to do; like putting their shoes on the wrong way, trying to tie their shoe-laces or having a full blown tantrum one minute and being little angels the next. There have been occasions when one of my sisters-in-law has recalled a funny incident involving Lisa. For instance, one night while we were staying over at her house, Dave and my brother had gone out to a pub, and we had assumed that Lisa just like Kevin was still fast asleep. My sister-in-law and I were sitting watching the telly, so when we heard a sort of muffled sound coming from the lobby we were slightly startled and wondered if a sneak thief had entered the house while we were engrossed in the programme we were watching.

We slowly opened the living-room door not knowing what we might see, only to be confronted with Lisa who had wrapped herself and covered most of the distance between the bathroom and the lobby with an extremely long strand of toilet tissue, just like the advert on the telly for Andrex Toilet

Tissue, but instead of a puppy doing the trailing of toilet tissue everywhere. It was my daughter who had done the deed. Lisa had clearly got up to use the toilet and wishing to wipe her bottom she had pulled at the roll but instead of detaching the amount she wanted she had not been able to figure out how to tear the piece off which resulted in her pulling more and more on the end and not being able to stop the rest of the roll from unravelling from its holder. So here was my little girl completely baffled by what had happened and not understanding why it was happening and too young to know how to put all that toilet paper back to where it ought to be. You can imagine the looks my sister-in-law and I exchanged knowing immediately what went wrong and trying not too upset Lisa by laughing at the state she had got herself into – just because she wanted to dry her bottom, like a good little girl. I swept her up and gave her a cuddle while my sister-in-law cleared up several feet of tissue. It is so good to have that memory to share, we don't talk about it every time we are together but it helps both of us to remember Lisa with a happy thought and not just thinking of her no longer being with us.

I think this is one of the saddest situations when our own parents and brothers and sisters don't share their memories of our children with us, because by not doing so they miss out in so much of the healing that recalling memories brings. Yes, I know, we all know, that it is excruciatingly hard to do this at first and it can cause countless tears to be shed, but as we have also all learned that it is in the remembering that we are able to hold on to them just a little and eventually we can recall naughty things they did too and not feel guilty that we chastised them, not realising how precious little time we would have them in our lives. It took me many years before I got any memories back about Lisa. All I could think of was the day I lost her. Nothing prior to that day would enter my mind. Yes, I remember every single thing about the day she died and can see it in my mind's eye how that day unfolded and the outcome, but that was it.

There were no happy recollections of stressful days of being a mother to two toddlers who were at that point both in nappies and trying to feed clothe and see to their wellbeing and Dave's. Everything seemed to be wiped out of my past existence and I did not know if any of it would return. I learned that this was a result of shock. Eventually, some good memories surfaced but just light hearted ones and it was years later when I could actually share times with others when Lisa had tantrums and we had arguments. There was the time I found that she had climbed into Kevin's cot. His cot was on wheels and in the same room was her single-bed. Lisa had pushed Kevin's cot over to the bed, climbed onto it and into the cot beside her little brother. Ordinarily this would not have been a problem, but when I found her she was in danger of falling on top of Kevin and despite him being a fairly robust toddler by this time, if she had landed on him, he would certainly have been seriously hurt. As a result of that incident they no longer were allowed to share the same bedroom. Lisa was given her own one further along the hallway, so that Kevin was nearer our room and we would be able to hear if she went into his room in future and attempted to get in beside him again.

It is possible; however, that there are bereaved parents who have found all the support they need from family members. A family that wants to keep the memory of the lost child alive within the family's collective memories. Sadly, for many others this is not the case. For many of us it is necessary to find outlets and people who do want to hear about our child before and since their death. This is why some of us have had to look for support and comfort from strangers, but these strangers can become more treasured then our closest friends or family.

It is not that we stop loving and wanting to be with those who have known us the longest. It is just that to enable us to live a worthwhile life without our child, we need to be with others who know instantly how we are feeling; where no words are needed, but who can physically and emotionally embrace our need to talk about our beloved children. We still have a deep seated love for our children and we need to find what to do with this love. We cannot give it to anyone else; because it is the love we will always feel for our children even though we can no longer share it with them. We cannot forget it. We cannot apportion it out and divide it among our other children or grandchildren. The only person it was for is the person who in no longer around.

So what can we do with it? We can hold on to it and use it to enable us to do something for our child even if that means getting up out of bed, putting one step in front of the other, picking up the remnants of our life and getting on with life. We knew our childrens' personalities, like no one else did, so we know how they would feel if their loss has caused us ongoing pain and sorrow. There is no denying that we do feel the pain and sorrow and for a while we should allow ourselves to do so, but, I believe, that the love we had and still have for our lost youngsters can and should be the impelling force which causes us to want to live, even with the pain of the loss, the agony of the longing and the missing. We have to accept that they have gone from this earth, but they will never be gone from our hearts and minds.

I hope my words can still bring comfort to those who have lost babies. I feel that it is hard to quantify the depth of pain felt at losing a child before they have had much time to live. Yet the bottom line is that we have all lost a child who was once our babe in arms and this is what unites all bereaved parents all over the world and it is such a unique pain for each of us that it is impossible for mere words to pacify our pain-ridden hearts.

Nevertheless, it is possible to move on through the turmoil. It isn't easy and there are many pitfalls in our paths. Life cannot be the same ever again. We cannot change what has happened, but we can grow through it and emerge new different, changed people. We can reach a time in our life when we can feel, once more, that it is good to be alive and be determined that nothing is going to deter us from living the life we choose, whether others approve of our choices or not. We can emerge from child loss stronger and able to deal with anything life has to throw at us. We can put that down to the strength our children have given us.

Yes, of course, it would have been better not to have suffered in this way, but we have and I feel that I want to make the best out of this 'new me' not because Lisa died, but because she had lived.

Chapter 10

Lessons Learned

One of the biggest insights I became aware of since Lisa died - is that the journey I had begun on that first day would never truly have an end. Initially, this was something I thought horrendous because as much as I missed her I could not see how I would be able to bear so much pain for the remainder of my life, however long that would be. Not horrendous in the sense that it was a burden to carry such a weight of grief, but in the sense of how any human-being could hope to deal with it. Yet the thought of parting with the pain of her loss was just as difficult to contemplate.

When we can't move on and we can't go back then we can become bogged down and remain in the quagmire that our lives have become. For some that is where they will stay. Others of us come to realise much to their dismay that they have begun

184

to move on from the day their child died. When this happens all sorts of unexpected emotions overwhelm us. We feel that moving forward is in some way a betrayal of our child and at least the pain we have is a tangible thing, despite it being so overbearing. We know it is real. In our hearts and minds we are struggling to come to accept what we do not wish to admit, that our daughters or sons cannot be with us in our homes ever again, but this is the reality.

I have come to know through my own journey that if we do not start to let go or do something to alleviate the crushing pain we feel then we are not allowing ourselves to experience other emotions such as love. The love we still have and will always have for our lost ones. We can perhaps then learn to enjoy the love they still hold for us. They will never be able to understand the love we had for them, but can our surviving children ever fully comprehend our love for them, either? The love the great majority of parents have for their own children can never be truly measured.

When I embarked on this 'road' of grief it felt like an endless homework assignment which would never be completed. No matter how I strived to find definitive answers I could not. It took me a long time to understand that there would be no absolute conclusion to my sorrow. There came a point when I thought that I did not really want it to be over and done with, not then and not yet now. I knew it still means Lisa has gone, from my life on earth, but in some way she has never really left me. Once I realised that in some ways she would always be near and that there was no possibility of re-writing history, I had to accept the reality of her loss and rebuild a life which eventually included, for me, having two more children.

Having Marc and Fiona threw up yet a further recognition; how could I possibly go back, even supposing I could? What do I do about my two youngest children? The truth is that if Lisa had lived

I cannot be sure if I would have had any more babies. I had my daughter and my son, the 'ideal' family as society might suggest. I had started to consider being sterilised so we would not add to our family. This was a sobering thought that came into my mind one day when I had been mulling over on how my life had panned out. I had to face the facts straight on – I had to put my loss into some kind of perspective. I had chosen to have more children and I am delighted that I did, they have enriched my life in so many various ways, so I do not regret for one second having the opportunity to add more children to our family. There were times while raising Marc and Fiona, I chose not to be so involved with supporting bereaved parents, as I believed my children deserved to have most of my time and attention. They did not ask to be born, but in having them they needed to know that they would always have first call on my love, nurturing and mothering.

Kevin, too, was growing into a well adjusted young man despite the many different schools and homes he had to adapt to each time Dave was moved to another place of work. He deserved some consistency in his life and so when we returned to Inverurie in 1993, I made the decision that we as a family would not be moving again. If Dave's employers wished to move him to somewhere else, the children and I would remain in Inverurie and he would commute, even if this meant he had to be away for weeks or months at a time. I felt that the children and especially Kevin deserved to have, from then on, a stable home life. Thankfully, this is the way things have worked out. Dave has not needed to move abroad only to travel away from home for business meetings from time to time. He was once offered a chance to work in the US, but I refused to go and he turned down the offer. It may have been good for his career, but throughout the previous 15 years I had moved for his career. Now, the children had to come first and I have never once regretted making this decision and I know our children have since benefited from having a stable childhood growing up in one location. Dave's career never really suffered that much and as a family I believe remaining in Inverurie, where we still live, was the right thing for us to do.

Being a writer means a lot of time is spent alone. But one of the benefits is that it could be done when the children were asleep or when they were at school; when they were out with their friends. Now that they are all adults it can be done any time I want to do it. I still prefer to do it when they are busy elsewhere, as I don't ever wish them to think that my writing is more precious to me than they are. Dave sometimes seemed to resent my writing, but he has to understand that it is and has been the saving of me since he refuses to talk about Lisa. He needs to accept that for me writing is as important in my dealing with her loss as burying his feelings is for him.

Now there are periods when the thought of her never enters my mind for days or weeks at a time. There are even occasions when I need to remind myself that an anniversary of hers is due, a birthday or some such occasion. What's more, I no longer feel guilty at having not had her at the forefront of my mind even though an anniversary is coming up. I put this down to the way our lives move on naturally. Then at other times think to myself that she would be in her thirties and that if she were still alive she might be living in a foreign country or we may have fallen out to such an extent that we talk only when the need arises. I think some people may believe that I have indeed gone insane but this is only another strategy I use to help me live my life without her. And if this helps me deal with a different aspect of Lisa's death then why should I not use it? I don't suggest others do the same; they have to find their own way of coping with their loss, if it helps them to do as I do they can.

After we settled back into Inverurie in April 1993, our new street had a lot of little girls in it and one or two small boys who readily became playmates for Fiona, who was now three years old.

Kevin and Marc struck it lucky too as there were boys in the street who were old enough for them to kick a ball with and so the children were out playing most days. I, too, had a ready made circle of friends as most of the mothers formed a baby-sitting circle; and with Dave settled back into an office routine life seemed to be ticking-over nicely.

Now that I had time to read the newspapers I kept being confronted with stories of young people losing their lives in road accidents and by other means. This prompted me to think again of supporting bereaved parents. I made an attempt at starting a house group, but it didn't work out. I did meet with one or two mothers whose children had died, but they preferred one to one meetings, rather than coming together. The meetings eventually petered out as both women needed different things from me and I found it hard to know how best to help each of them.

Subsequently I decided to find out where the next national gathering was to be held for the

Scottish Forum, the branch of The Compassionate Friends based in Scotland. It was being held in Perth so I booked myself a place for their weekend in May 2002. I felt that if I wanted to continue to help other parents with their losses I had to become more involved again with the organisation that had helped me to find my way and stay on the right path which had enabled me to deal with any unforeseen hurdles.

It was also about this time my friend's daughter's cystic fibrosis condition started to deteriorate. Slowly she was losing lung capacity, despite the numerous concoctions of drugs and physiotherapy she received and initially making a good recovery after a double lung transplant. Time ran out for her and she passed away in 2003.

I wasn't sure if I would be strong enough to support my friend so I wanted to make sure that if my friend needed me to be strong and a good support for her I had somewhere to go if I needed supporting, too. As things have turned out my friend and I don't need to talk, but when we do we are able to chat fondly of our two daughters and sometimes shed an odd tear. Importantly we know we are there for each other and knowing that is often all we need.

Words can never be completely sufficient to express the deep seated longing in the depth of a bereaved parent's heart and sometimes the best thing to give us comfort for our wounds is silence. Simply just sitting with another bereaved parent is all we need. Our friends who have not lost a child can do this too. They do not need to say a word just sit silently beside us and allow us to mull over things and once we are ready we will smile a gentle smile and be glad that you were strong enough to sit with us instead of leaving us sitting alone and feeling isolated.

After that first Scottish Forum a friend of mine on the committee invited me to join in the preparation for the next Gathering in May 2004. As these weekends are about bereaved parents coming together in a conference setting, we have chosen to call them 'Gathering' which is a much kinder word than a cold empty word like 'conference'. We do not come together to have business meetings or to discuss better ways of working together. The business and organisation of the Gatherings take place at a number of committee meetings held prior to the weekend of the Gathering.

The weekends are then given over to offering support and advice to all the bereaved parents attending. Various discussion groups are run usually with a maximum of twelve led by a bereaved parent who has coped with his or her loss for some years and is now willing to share what they have learned with those just beginning the arduous task of learning what it means to be a grieving parent. Most groups vary from year to year but sadly some are run year in year out as there are always newly bereaved who need those groups. The groups which are always made available are: A Mother's Grief; A Father's Grief and a group for parents whose children have taken their own lives.

Others which run most years are: Death of an Adult Child; Death of a Child through Murder, and Sudden Death. Various others are arranged as the need arises and at the requests of parents.

When, 'One step at a time/Mourning a Child' was published. It sold very well to begin with but I soon realised that it was not possible for me to get behind the book as much as I could have done. I believe that it would have sold well throughout the world, if I had been able to get more involved with its promotion.

I knew that while Marc and Kevin were growing up and could probably have coped with me travelling around pushing my book, Fiona was reaching an age when she really needed her mum to be around. She was approaching puberty and I realised that if I went around promoting a book about how much I missed one daughter. I risked the chance of missing out in the care of the daughter I do have. (For bereaved parents 'closure' and its meaning of an end to grieving is wrong – as it feels like it never stops.) Consequently, I chose to step back from the book and to stay at home and enjoy raising Fiona as well as her brothers. I have never regretted making this decision for a single day since.

The year 2011 saw Fiona turn 21, Marc 26 and Kevin settled in marriage to our beautiful daughter-in-law, Ruth. Dave is semi-retired having taken voluntary redundancy in 2009. I am now willing and able to re-launch my task of using writing to offer support to bereaved parents and give advice to any agency which wants to help such parents. Not as I have said before and will say time and again, to gain fame or fortune for myself. Only what I hoped to achieve when I set out on the road to publication, thirty years ago, to say to fellow grieving parents there is a way out of the abyss that you have found yourselves in. It is possible to rebuild a life worth living and it will be possible for you to one day smile, laugh and even be glad that you are still alive.

However, first you need to want to do this, but if you do not then that's okay too – we are all entitled to grieve as we need to and not as someone else believes we should. This my friend, Molly, in Brazil could never grasp and why should she be able to, since it is only by losing a child that you come to know the full understanding of what the death of your own child means to your life. Yet there can be life after the loss of our children if we want to search for it. It might take a long time to find and some may never find it to their complete satisfaction, but through agencies like The Compassionate Friends, parents need not do the seeking on their own.

Rather than seeing my return to The Compassionate Friends as a backward step and an admission that I was still not strong enough to cope on my own with my loss. I saw it as my way of using the experiences, both of being supported by them at one stage in my grief and then going it alone for a while. These are strengths which I was again willing to use to support parents who were not as far along in their 'journey through their losses'. The fact that I knew now the difference the support made helped to show me, if no one else, the real value of finding the right type of support, something no parent expects to have to do from such an agency.

It did mean that sometimes I had to revisit my early painful days when the loss first occurred, but this was necessary to enable me to be of use to and to empathise with those parents who were newly bereaved. It was not easy, though I think it did allow me to face things which I might have glossed over at the time and was now strong enough to deal with. There are times in the past thirty years when I have wondered if there could have been a better, different way for me to handle my loss. There have been times when I thought of just walking away from everything and leaving bereaved parents for some one else to support. I could not and I have come to realize that it is what makes my life real. It is what for whatever reason I have been given to do.

However, it is not my task alone. There are many others doing the same. Countless other grieving mums and dads who having found support for themselves are waiting with open hearts and arms to embrace those parents who are just beginning the journey and need the understanding which only another such parent can offer. I know that the word 'journey' is now very over-used. And in some ways it is just too simple a word to describe the experiences which many grieving parents encounter. Perhaps, 'education' would be a more accurate word to use. Because when children die the only way for all their parents to come to terms with the loss, in my mind, is to learn to live without their children and like starting school as infants we can only do this slowly and methodically. For that is the only way, I believe, to deal with our losses.

The enormity of our loss is right there at the very start and in many cases it will be the disbelief that protects us from the complete impact at the time, but when this lifts and reality sets in, which could be days, weeks or even years later, it is then we might seek a way to deal with the loss. Some will never find it. And others will only succeed because they are able to meet with other bereaved parents once in a while.

Did I ever doubt that what I was doing was the right way for me to deal with my own grief? Did I consider that I had read the signs wrong and that I just believed in false hopes and promises? The answer to both these questions has to be, yes. I mulled over these questions on many occasions about why I felt so driven to have my story published. After all once I had found The Compassionate Friends in some ways I had the audience I sought, but I knew that this wasn't the end goal of what I hoped to achieve through my writing. I hadn't aspired to become a bereaved mother any more than it was a dream to be a writer, but I did become both and I felt there had to be some reason behind these two events in my life.

Therefore, I was going to need something outside myself to enable me to learn to live without Lisa. For this I had to put my trust in God to provide me with the support I needed to make sense out of an atrocious situation that I was in. Something which happens on television and in the movies had actually come to my door. I could not have come this far if I had not believed that my source of help came from God and that through His support I found that my Christian faith was strengthened. Without my faith along with my writing and the friends I have made within The Compassionate Friends, my life would have remained an empty shell.

I might well still have managed to stay alive, but it would not have been living in the true sense of the word, but merely existing. I do believe that God could have stopped Lisa from drowning, if He had so wished. I do not know why He did not, but since

He didn't I felt justified in demanding that He help me cope with her loss. Why did I not turn away and refuse to have anything to do with a God who can allow me to suffer in this way? Again I cannot fully understand, but I need His support to be able to live without her and while I am doing this, I might as well make good use of my time. To offer some kind of consolation to parents in the same situation who need help in their grief.

I have come to think that Lisa was never meant to live longer than she did. It doesn't matter that I was unaware of this while she was with me. It wasn't God's fault that I had assumed that she would be well educated, grow up, have a family of her own, and live a full and wholesome life. None of us know, except those diagnosed with a terminal illness, when our lives will end. We live for tomorrow instead of the day we have now. We make plans for years down the line, but the truth is few of us know how many todays we still have. The same might be said about the lives of our children.

No one is guaranteed to live forever. The surest thing about being alive is that one day we will each die. This may not be of much comfort to bereaved parents, but on the other hand it means that one day we may be reunited with our children when it is the right time for us to leave this world. However, I feel, it is worth stating anyway.

Our children are safe where they are. Nothing can harm them again and it is only our love for them that causes us to miss them as we do. These truths, I know, don't really help to ease our pain, though they might help a little. For me facing these truths did help. It stopped me grieving for the things which were never going to happen in a future which Lisa was never destined have. She was not ever going to start Primary School, or to go on her first date, marry and have children. These were all things which I had foreseen for her, not what was going to happen. They also showed me what I would miss. As a result, I guess, the loss of these had to be dealt with. Yet I had used my imagination to picture her grown-up and that was my fault and nobody else's. And I suppose I have to admit these are all the things I do grieve about, in addition to all the other things that happen in the course of a family's lifetime.

It is clear from the last few paragraphs that I am still wading through the regret of the lost times which I had hoped to have with Lisa; and that I hope to experience with my other children. It also demonstrated that I am still learning to live without her and this is all any of us can do. There are bound to be things in the future which will only serve to emphasize what we lost on the day Lisa died. It is only natural to feel sad at these times and wonder 'what if', but we need to be strong and walk tall and be proud of how we have managed to survive, though really wishing we could lie down and sleep for ever. However, if our kids could see us, they would be happy that we were glad to be their mums and dads for however short that time had been and were slowly managing to cope without them.

So would I do the same things again, make the same choices as I did? There are a few things I do regret and those were the times when I thought I knew how to help a grieving parent when they had chosen not to become involved with The Compassionate Friends and I was more persistent than I ought to have been. However, over all I think I would do the same things all over again, as I believe I did the right things to help me deal with Lisa's loss and I have done so many things I could not have envisaged doing if she had never been in my life.

Of course, I would have preferred not to have lost her and add to our family as well, but alas my life took another route. I had to deal with the hand I was dealt in the best and the only 'right' way for me as an individual. If writing about my 'journey' can serve others in theirs then that's all I hoped could arise out of my own very personal loss, for my love of Lisa.

The end.